DK EYEWITNESS

TOP **10**
ITALIAN LAKES

T0047126

Top 10 Italian Lakes Highlights

The Top 10 of Everything

CONTENTS

Italian Lakes Area by Area

Streetsmart

Within each Top 10 list in this book, no hierarchy of quality or popularity is implied. All 10 are, in the editor's opinion, of roughly equal merit.

Title page, front cover and spine *The picturesque village of Varenna on Lake Como* ***Back cover, clockwise from top left*** *Galleria Vittorio Emanuele II; Sirmione; Borromeo Palace, Isola Bella; Varenna; a waterfall in Nesso, Lake Como*

The rapid rate at which the world is changing is constantly keeping the DK Eyewitness team on our toes. While we've worked hard to ensure that this edition of Italian Lakes is accurate and up-to-date, we know that opening hours alter, standards shift, prices fluctuate, places close and new ones pop up in their stead. So, if you notice we've got something wrong or left something out, we want to hear about it. Please get in touch at **travelguides@dk.com**

Welcome to
The Italian Lakes

Majestic views and snowcapped mountains have drawn the rich and famous to the Italian Lakes since ancient Roman times. Many writers and artists have spent time in this area, their works inspired by its dramatic beauty. With DK Eyewitness Top 10 Italian Lakes, it's yours to explore.

It's little wonder that film directors regularly take advantage of the region's ready-made film sets, often making use of the area's grand historic **villas**. Outside, exuberant **gardens** burst with vegetation, which flourishes thanks to a surprisingly mild micro-climate. These villas and their gardens are among the world's most impressive – true works of architectural and horticultural art.

No less important to the landscape are the countless **lakeside villages**, their enchanting historic centres punctuated by landmark bell towers and picturesque harbours. Idyllic waterfront promenades are lined with pavement cafés, perfect for a lazy afternoon.

For the more dynamic, the lakes are also ideal natural arenas for **watersports**. Thanks to regular wind patterns, they offer safe or challenging conditions for beginners and experts alike. The mountains provide a plethora of sports options, too, both in summer and winter, and walkers have a surfeit of choice, from pleasant lakeside footpaths to tough mountain treks. There's also plenty of culture, with several outstanding **cities of art** a stone's throw away.

Whether you're visiting for a weekend or a week, our Top 10 guide brings together the best of everything the Italian Lakes can offer, from the elegance of **Lake Como** and **Lake Maggiore**, to relaxing **Lake Iseo** and lively **Lake Garda**. The guide has useful tips throughout, from seeking out what's free to places off the beaten track, plus seven easy-to-follow itineraries designed to tie together a clutch of sights in a short space of time. Add inspiring photography and detailed maps, and you've got the essential pocket-sized travel companion. **Enjoy the book, and enjoy the Italian Lakes.**

Clockwise from top: **La Scala in Milan, Casa di Giulietta in Verona, beautiful town of Lovere, Varenna, Renaissance art in Verona, Roman architecture in Brescia, Lake Garda**

Exploring the Italian Lakes

There is so much to see in the Italian Lakes area – each place deserving time to absorb its individual atmosphere – that a weekend visit is best dedicated to just one or two of the lakes. A week is ideal for getting an idea of the area as a whole, although visitors will undoubtedly want to stay longer.

Two Days at the Italian Lakes

Day ❶
MORNING
Spend the day on Lake Maggiore's **Isole Borromee** *(see pp12–13)*. Take the ferry from **Stresa** *(see p71)* to Isola Bella, visiting the villa and gardens before the crowds. Cross to Isola dei Pescatori for lunch at **Hotel Verbano** *(see p75)*. Book a lakeside terrace table.

AFTERNOON
Head to Isola Madre with your combined islands ticket, and explore the lush gardens before returning for the evening in Stresa, the pearl of Lake Maggiore.

Day ❷
MORNING
Start in **Como** *(see pp18–19)*. After visiting the **Duomo** *(see p78)*, take the funicular from the waterfront to **Brunate** *(see p77)*. Walk to the Volta Lighthouse and admire the views, then return to Brunate for lunch.

AFTERNOON
Back in Como, hop on a ferry to **Bellagio** and make the most of a Centro Lago ferry

Key
━━ Two-day itinerary
━━ Seven-day itinerary

ticket, spending the afternoon hopping between villages, particularly **Lenno**, **Varenna** and **Menaggio** *(see pp28–9)*.

Seven Days at the Italian Lakes

Day ❶
Spend the day in the historic city of **Verona** *(see pp26–7)*. Explore its Renaissance architecture and

Malcesine, on Lake Garda, is dominated by a medieval castle.

Verona's Roman Arena provides an unforgettable setting for opera performances.

0 km   25
0 miles   25

Lake Iseo — Monte Isola — ergamo — Malcesine — Monte Baldo — Lake Garda ❷ — Punta San Vigilio — Tenuta Canova — ❸ — Sirmione — Valpolicella — ITALY — Verona ❶

Lake Maggiore is dotted with charming villages.

maybe end the day with an opera at the Roman Arena (last-minute tickets are sometimes available).

Day ❷
Cross the **Valpolicella** area *(see p91)* on your way to **Lake Garda** *(see pp90–93)*, and stop at **Tenuta Canova** *(see p59)* to try some of the local wines. Head north for a swim and lunch at **Punta San Vigilio** *(see p51)*, then continue to **Malcesine** *(see p92)*. See the castle and take the cable car up **Monte Baldo** *(see p55)*, then retrace your steps, continuing to **Sirmione** *(see pp34–5)* for a sunset boat trip.

Day ❸
Set off early for **Lake Iseo** *(see pp32–3)* and catch the ferry to **Monte Isola** *(see p85)*. Stretch your legs with a walk up to Madonna della Ceriola, followed by a lunch of lake fish. Later, make your way to **Bergamo** *(see pp30–31)*, explore the **upper town** *(see p86)* and take the funicular to **San Vigilio** *(see p85)* for dinner.

Day ❹
Move on to **Milan** *(see pp22–3)*, indulge in some window-shopping and visit the remarkable **Duomo** *(see pp24–5)*, including the roof terrace. Later in the day, relax and refuel at the **Navigli District** *(see p100)*.

Day ❺
Head to **Como** *(see pp18–19)*, and follow Day 2 of the two-day itinerary.

Day ❻
Dedicate the day to **Lake Maggiore** *(see pp14–15)*, with a foray into Switzerland at **Ascona** *(see p73)*, then stopping at **Cannobio** *(see p72)* on your way to **Stresa** *(see p71)*.

Day ❼
The day starts with a visit to **Isola Bella** and **Isola dei Pescatori** *(see pp12–13)*. Next, return to the mainland and travel to the western-most of the lakes, **Lake Orta** *(see p69)*, for a relaxing end to the week at **Orta San Giulio** *(see pp16–17)*.

Top 10 Italian Lakes Highlights

Colourful houses in Menaggio, on
the western shore of Lake Como

🔟 Italian Lakes Highlights

The spectacular natural beauty of the Italian Lakes region, sheltering under the Alps, is matched by its historical legacy. Attractive lake villages and pretty towns offer a variety of fine art, architecture and cuisine, as well as opportunities for walking, cycling and watersports.

1 Isole Borromee

The gardens and villas of Isola Bella and Isola Madre, plus the fishing village vibe of Isola dei Pescatori, make these Lake Maggiore islands a must-see *(see pp12–13)*.

2 Northern Lake Maggiore

Italy melts into Switzerland at the northern end of the lake. The area's peculiar microclimate creates stunning displays of flora *(see pp14–15)*.

Locarno • Bellinzona
Lake Como
Northern Lake ❷ Centro Lago
Maggiore and its Villages ❼
Isole Borromee ❶ Lecco •
Orta San ❸ Varese • ❹ Como
Giulio Tradate •
Borgomanero •
Busto Monza •
Arsizio •
Rho • ❺ Milan
Novara •
Abbiategrasso • Melegnano •
Lodi

3 Orta San Giulio

This honey-coloured village on Lake Orta is nestled between the quiet woods of its Sacro Monte (Holy Mountain) and the lake *(see pp16–17)*.

4 Como

Wrapped around a bay at the southern end of Lake Como, the historic silk-producing town of Como features a grand cathedral and cobbled streets within a medieval wall *(see pp18–19)*.

5 Milan

Famous as a hub of fashion and design, Milan also features a magnificent Gothic cathedral and a host of museums *(see pp22–5)*.

6 Verona

Just east of Lake Garda, romantic Verona blends ancient streets, historical buildings and fine food and wine *(see pp26–7).*

7 Centro Lago and its Villages

Bellagio, with its stepped streets, sits at the centre of Lake Como, where the three branches of the lake meet *(see pp28–9).*

8 Bergamo

Ancient walls surround the upper town, while vineyards tumble down the hillside to the 19th-century lower town *(see pp30–31).*

9 Lake Iseo

Dominated by the Monte Isola island, Lake Iseo offers waterside villages, natural beauty and cultural attractions, plus great food and wine *(see pp32–3).*

10 Sirmione and Southern Lake Garda

The resort of Sirmione juts out into southern Lake Garda. Nearby lakeside villages have ancient centres, Grand Hotels and beaches *(see pp34–5).*

TOP 10 ⭐ Isole Borromee

Near Stresa is a cluster of islands called Isole Borromee. Isola Bella is the most striking, with its intricate Italianate garden, while Isola Madre, the largest, has landscaped botanical gardens that are a joy to explore. Both islands also have remarkable palaces. The third island, Isola dei Pescatori, is an authentic fishing village, while the tiny Isolotto della Malghera has little more than a beach.

1 Isola Bella

It is from the water that visitors can truly appreciate the concept to transform this island into an architectural master-piece resembling a ship. The tiered garden (above) represents the stern and the palace, the prow.

2 Palazzo Borromeo, Isola Bella

Highlights of this Baroque palace include the grand ballroom, adorned with Classical statues, and the pale-pink and stucco bedroom where Napoleon stayed with his wife Josephine.

4 Teatro Massimo, Isola Bella

This spot, marking the highest point of the Isola Bella gardens, is an explosion of statues and obelisks. The views over the lake and mountains beyond are superb.

3 Grottoes, Isola Bella

The walls and ceilings of this series of rooms (left), intended as a cool retreat during the hot summer months, are entirely encrusted with pebbles, shells, marble, stucco and mother-of-pearl, creating an unusual cave-like effect.

Isole Borromee

1.2 km (2 miles)

Isola dei Pescatori

Isola Bella

Stresa

6 Botanical Gardens, Isola Madre

Peacocks **(left)** and parrots roam freely in these gardens, which are famous for the flowering of the many azaleas, camellias and wisteria.

7 Gardens, Isola Bella

These Italianate gardens rise in a pyramid of ten terraces. White peacocks wander among rare and exotic plants, and topiary is interspersed with statues and balustrades.

8 Isola dei Pescatori

This island has the vibe of an authentic fishing village. Wander the cobbled lanes, visit the 11th-century San Vittore church, then stop at one of the many restaurants.

AN ISLAND RETREAT

A fifth island, Isolino di San Giovanni, is not open to the public. This, too, was acquired in the 17th century by the Borromeo family. More recently, from 1927 to 1952, it served as the residence of celebrated orchestral conductor Arturo Toscanini.
The island is just off the shore at Pallanza and can be seen from the lakeside promenade.

10 Isolotto della Malghera

This tiny island, also known as "island of the lovers", is midway between Isola dei Pescatori and Isola Bella. There's a little beach that can be reached by water taxi or rental boat.

5 Palazzo Borromeo, Isola Madre

The first Borromeo palace built on these islands, this structure dates from the 16th century. While modest in comparison to its counterpart on Isola Bella, it has an appealing interior featuring *trompe l'oeil* decorations, plus collections of antique dolls and marionettes.

9 Flemish Tapestries, Isola Bella

Seven 16th-century Flemish tapestries **(above)** are housed in a gallery within the palace. The vivid designs include unicorns, lions and birds.

NEED TO KNOW

MAP J3 ▪ 0323 933 478 ▪ www.isoleborromee.it

Isola Bella & Isola Madre: open late Mar–late Oct: 9am–5:30pm daily; book ahead for guided tours

Adm Isola Bella €18; Isola Madre €15; combined ticket on the same day €25; free for Royal Horticultural Society cardholders

Isola dei Pescatori: open year-round

▪ Refreshments are available on the larger islands, but not on Isolotto della Malghera.

▪ Ferries run from various points on the mainland, Stresa being the nearest.

🔟 ⭐ Northern Lake Maggiore

Lake Maggiore (also called Verbano) narrows at its northern tip with steep mountain ranges pushing in on the resorts and lakeside towns. Italy merges into Switzerland for the final loop of the lake. Attractive Italian villages dot the area, while further ahead there are well-established Swiss holiday resorts. The climate around the lake is ideal for sailing and windsurfing and also encourages banks of camellias, rhododendrons and palm trees that line the shores.

2 Locarno

This Swiss resort has been welcoming visitors since Roman times. Highlights include the 14th-century Castello Visconteo (see p43; **left**) and art in the Casa Rusca.

3 Cannero Riviera

In a corner of the western shore, this pretty resort village has a blue-flag beach and a boating harbour.

1 Orrido di Sant'Anna, Cannobio

At the start of Val Cannobio, this is a spectacular gorge marked by a medieval church and a restaurant. The pebbly river beach makes an ideal picnic spot.

4 Ascona

Galleries and craft shops line the cobbled streets that lead back from picturesque Piazza Motta at the lakefront in this Swiss town **(below)**. Ascona is a big attraction for artists.

Northern Lake Maggiore

Locarno
Ascona
Porto Ronco
Gerra
Pino
Cannobio
Maccagno
Cannero Riviera
Luino
Lake Maggiore

5 Lake Maggiore Express

The Lake Maggiore Express is an unforgettable round trip that combines a boat on Lake Maggiore, the spectacular Centovalli Railway and a fast train back to the lakeshore. This is a good-value way to explore the mountains and take in the beautiful scenery around the lake.

6 Windsurfing, Pino

Just short of the border with Switzerland, on the eastern shore of Maggiore, Pino offers many windsurfing **(above)** and kitesurfing opportunities. There are courses available for all levels, plus board hire.

7 Santuario della Pietà, Cannobio

On the waterfront, the lovely 16th-century Santuario della Pietà was built on the orders of Cardinal Carlo Borromeo when the village was spared the worst of a plague that decimated the local population.

8 Isole di Brissago

The tiny islands of Sant'Apollinare and San Pancrazio that lie just offshore in Switzerland comprise the Isole di Brissago. San Pancrazio, *(see p44)* the larger island, has a botanical garden.

9 Wednesday Market, Luino

Bus- and ferry-loads of visitors head for the weekly market at Luino, on the eastern shore of the lake. The stalls have something for everyone.

A FAREWELL TO ARMS

Ernest Hemingway's World War I novel *A Farewell to Arms* is set on the Italian Front, in Milan and on Lake Maggiore. American ambulance driver Frederic Henry drinks martinis in Stresa before being reunited with British nurse Catherine Barkley. To escape the Italian authorities, they row through the night to cross the border into Switzerland.

10 Sunday Market, Cannobio

One of the lake's most attractive villages is taken over every Sunday morning by a market **(above)** along the waterfront. Stalls offer everything from local produce to leather goods and clothing.

NEED TO KNOW

Locarno Tourist Office: **MAP L1**; Piazza Stazione

Cannero Riviera Tourist Office: **MAP K2**; Via Angelo Orsi 1

Ascona Tourist Office: **MAP K1**; Viale Papio 5

Lake Maggiore Express: **MAP K2**; round-trip passes (€34 for 1 day and €44 for 2 days) and tickets are available from ferry companies, train stations, tourist offices and travel agents around the lake; www.lago maggioreexpress.it

Windsurfing, Pino: **MAP K2**; Scuola Windsurf La Darsena; Corso Europa 5, 339 296 2927; open Jun–Sep

Isole di Brissago: **MAP K2**; Ferry from Porto Ronco, Locarno, Brissago & Ascona; open Mar–Oct: 9am–6pm; adm

Wednesday market, Luino: **MAP K3**; Via Piero Chiara

Sunday market, Cannobio: **MAP K2**; Via A Giovanola

■ In Switzerland, petrol is cheaper.

TOP 10 ⭐ Orta San Giulio

Lake Orta (also known as Cusio) lies entirely within the region of Piemonte. The westernmost of the Italian lakes, Lake Orta is flanked by hills and steep slopes of chestnut trees. The highlight is the lakeside village of Orta San Giulio – a string of cobbled lanes and attractive Liberty villas. The UNESCO World Heritage Site of Sacro Monte, an atmospheric sanctuary with spectacular views, lies above the village, while just offshore sits the island of Isola San Giulio, offering a retreat from the modern world.

① Isola San Giulio

The quiet island of San Giulio (above), west of Orta San Giulio, is home to a community of nuns. The 19th-century Benedictine seminary and a graceful bell tower dominate the skyline.

② Wednesday Market

Since 1228, Orta's weekly market has taken over the main waterside square of Piazza Motta, offering a host of fresh local produce including vegetables, fruit, salami, cheese and meat.

③ Piazza Motta

The village alleyways wind around the heart of Orta – the Piazza Motta (left) – a broad piazza dotted with cafés and lakeside benches. An ideal spot to watch the world go by.

⑤ Il Trenino

This charming little motorized train (above) takes the puff out of Orta's steep gradients. A trip between the hill-top tourist office and Piazza Motta is covered in 30 minutes.

④ Palazzo della Comunità

Built in 1582, this lovely palace in the main square is reached by an external staircase. The court and council room is decorated by the Baroque fresco *Madonna and Francesco and Giulio*.

⑧ Basilica di San Giulio

The island-church was founded in the first century AD, but the current building is from the 10th century, with Baroque touch-ups. Frescoes line the walls and ceiling **(left)**, and the marble pulpit is covered with allegorical carvings.

ST JULIUS (SAN GIULIO)

According to legend, Julius left his native Greece and went to Orta in AD 390 in order to escape persecution as a Christian. The island was said to be guarded by serpents and dragons and no one was willing to row him to it. Julius used his cape as a sail and single-handedly rid the island of the beasts and built the church that houses his remains.

⑩ Sacro Monte di San Francesco

Winding through the nature reserve above town is the Sacro Monte (Holy Mountain) path, lined with 20 chapels with impressive 17th- to 18th-century terra-cotta works from the life of St Francis of Assisi.

⑥ Leon d'Oro

In a region full of idyllic locations, it still does not get much better than at the Leon d'Oro. The restaurant, part of a family-run hotel, has a lovely lakeside terrace.

⑨ Via Olina

Narrow, cobbled Via Olina is Orta's main thoroughfare. A pleasant mix of eclectic boutiques and delicatessens offer souvenirs to take home.

⑦ Rowing on the Lake

Scenic Lake Orta is great for a spot of rowing. Boatmen on Piazza Motta rent out rowing boats by the hour.

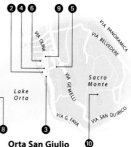

Orta San Giulio

NEED TO KNOW

MAP J4

Orta San Giulio Tourist Office: Via Panoramica 2; 0322 905 163; Nov–Mar: closed Mon–Fri

Isola San Giulio: Boats from Piazza Motta every 10 mins 9am–6:30pm

Il Trenino: Via Panoramica; Opening times vary, check website; www.treninodiorta.com

Leon d'Oro: Piazza Motta 42; 0322 911 991

Basilica di San Giulio: open Apr–Oct: 9:45am–6pm daily; Nov–Mar: 9:30am–noon & 2–5pm daily; www.benedettineisolasangiulio.org

Sacro Monte di San Francesco: 0322 90149; Chapels: open summer: 9:30am–6pm Mon–Fri (to 6:30pm Sat & Sun); winter: 9:30am–4pm Mon–Fri (to 4:30pm Sat & Sun)

■ The local *gastronomia* on the central Piazza Motta makes excellent panini.

TOP 10 ⭐ Como

At the foot of the Alps, this lakeside town has been an important place commercially and politically since pre-Roman times. In the late 1800s, Como became a wealthy backwater, combining textile manufacturing with its role as staging post for the many tourists here to enjoy the delights of the lake. The old town is a maze of cobbled streets leading down to the palm-lined waterfront promenade.

NEED TO KNOW

MAP M4

Tourist Office: Piazza Cavour 17; 031 269 712; open daily

Villa Olmo: Via Cantoni; 031 576 169; open 10am–6pm Tue–Sun; gardens: 7am–11pm daily (Oct–Mar: to 7pm)

Duomo: Piazza del Duomo; open 10:30am–5pm Mon–Sat, 1–4:30pm Sun

San Fedele: Piazza San Fedele; open 8am–noon & 3:30–7pm daily

Museo Civico: Piazza Medaglie d'Oro 1; open 8:30am–12:30pm & 2:30–5pm Tue–Thu, 8:30am–noon Fri

Villa Geno: Viale Geno 12; open 10am–6/9pm daily

Sant'Abbondio: Via Sant'Abbondio; open 8am–5pm daily (summer to 6pm)

Funicular: Piazza de Gasperi; open 6am–10:30pm daily (Jun–mid-Sep: to midnight); return ticket €5.70

1 Villa Olmo

The 18th-century Villa Olmo has sumptuous, frescoed interiors **(above)** that host temporary exhibitions. The villa's formal lakefront gardens make a pleasant public park.

2 Boat Trips

Regular ferries link the lakeside villages. Hydrofoil express services and leisurely sightseeing cruises are also on offer. Boat services from Como **(below)** run all year round, with a reduced timetable in winter.

3 Duomo

Como's cathedral **(below)** is a harmonious mix of architectural styles, including a Gothic façade, a Renaissance rose window and a Baroque dome *(see p78)*.

Lake
Como

PIAZZA
CAVOUR

Como

6 San Fedele
Founded in 914, Como's former cathedral has a striking octagonal apse and 14th-century frescoes, as well as an ornate door decorated with various portly figures and a griffin.

7 Museo Civico
Housed in two elegant *palazzi*, the Museo Civico displays Roman artifacts **(left)** and memorabilia from the Italian Unification period.

8 Villa Geno
A 30-minute stroll around the bay from Como brings you to the grounds of Villa Geno, where the splendid fountain on the waterfront is a must see.

A CENTRE FOR SILK

Como has been Europe's most important silk centre since the 16th century. Family-run factories here specialize in creating high-quality, low-run merchandise that is demanded by the world's leading fashion houses such as Gucci, Versace and Hermès.

4 Brunate
At the top of the funicular track, little Brunate offers fabulous views across the lake, and is the starting point of many trails into the hills. Cafés and restaurants here are especially busy for Sunday lunch.

5 Palazzo Terragni
Designed by architect Giuseppe Terragni as the local Fascist Party headquarters in the 1930s, this palace is seen as the definitive example of Rationalist architecture for its functional, light beauty.

9 Sant'Abbondio
Consecrated to the patron saint of Como in 1095, this attractive Romanesque church has colourful Byzantine frescoes adorning its walls.

10 Funicular
Como's funicular train **(above)** goes up and down between the town's villas and gardens. The funicular station is in the northeast corner of Como. It takes 7 minutes to reach Brunate at the top of the hill.

TOP 10 ★ Milan

Milan is Italy's economic heart: the centre of banking, publishing and industry, as well as a fashion capital of the world. Guarding the route from Rome to Central Europe, it has always been a strategic commercial hub. Milan was bombed during World War II, resulting in a mix of architectural styles, but it is a beguiling place, with many treasures amid its medieval lanes and 19th-century arcades.

La Scala ①
The world-famous opera house (right) opened its opulent interior to the public in 1778. The opera season starts on 7 December, the feast of the city's patron saint St Ambrose. Information on tickets is available from the website.

② Sant'Ambrogio
Founded in the 4th century by Milan's patron saint, St Ambrose, this church (below) was rebuilt in the 12th century. The capitals of the columns in the atrium feature horses, dragons and other beasts.

③ Navigli District
A buzzing bar and restaurant scene has grown up around two of the city's remaining canals. There is a bric-a-brac market here on the last Sunday of the month.

⑤ Quadrilatero d'Oro
The sleek displays in the windows of top fashion labels are a feast for the eyes. Prices may be prohibitive but every style and taste is catered for.

④ Castello Sforzesco
The castle complex was built between 1360 and 1370 by the rulers of Milan, the Visconti, and continued by their successors, the Sforza. Now a museum, it houses Michelangelo's *Rondanini Pietà* statue.

Milan

Previous pages The Gothic façade of Milan's Duomo

MILAN'S CANALS
First developed in the 12th century for goods transport and defence, Milan's canal network was gradually added to until the city was linked by waterway with the lakes and Switzerland to the north, and with the River Po and the Adriatic Sea to the south. In the early 20th century, the canals were built over for hygiene and mobility.

8 Pinacoteca di Brera

This gallery (see p99) holds the most important collection of Northern Italian art in the world. Highlights include masterpieces by Raphael **(above)** and Mantegna.

6 Galleria Vittorio Emanuele II

This grand 19th-century shopping arcade **(above)** links the cathedral square with the opera house. The mosaics under the glass dome celebrate the Unification of Italy.

7 Duomo

The third-largest church in Europe, Milan's Gothic Duomo **(below)** took almost six centuries to complete. Clamber over the roof for a dizzying look over its marble spires and statues, and to enjoy views of the city's skyline.

9 Parco Sempione

The castle's old hunting grounds are Milan's largest green space, with lawns, cafés, the Triennale (see p99), a children's playground and a library.

10 The Last Supper

Leonardo da Vinci's *The Last Supper* was painted on a refectory wall at the Santa Maria delle Grazie monastery (see p99).

Duomo

1 Scurolo di San Carlo
The bejewelled remains of San Carlo Borromeo, the city's 16th-century cardinal and champion of the poor, are laid out in the crypt. He lies in a crystal coffin clothed in pontifical regalia and a silver mask.

Duomo floorplan

The Scurolo di San Carlo, in the crypt

2 Nail from the Cross
A red light on the ceiling marks the cathedral's most prized possession – a nail from Christ's Cross, today preserved in the reliquary. On the Saturday preceding 14 September, a complicated system of pulleys lowers the nail down to be paraded by the Bishop of Milan.

3 St Bartholomew Flayed
One of the cathedral's strangest statues is the oddly beguiling and gruesome carving of *St Bartholomew Flayed* by Marco d'Agrate (1562). The saint stands calmly with his skin flung over his shoulder and has fascinatingly accurate knees and toenails hanging lifelessly.

4 Battistero Paleocristiano
A narrow staircase leads down to the site discovered during work on the metro in the 1950s. There are the remains of Roman baths and a 4th-century basilica, as well as the baptistry where St Ambrose baptized St Augustine in AD 387.

5 Roof Terraces
One of the highlights of any visit to Milan is a wander amid the soaring white pinnacles and statues on the cathedral's marble terraces. Take the lift, or walk up the steps; follow the signs for the roof (*Salita alle terrazze*). On a clear day, there are fantastic views over the rooftops of Milan to the Alps.

6 La Madonnina
The Madonnina, or Little Madonna, is the gilded statue perched right on the very top of the cathedral, and stands 108 m (354 ft) above ground. The original statue was placed here in 1774, and was subsequently restored in 1967.

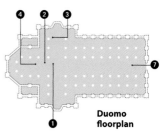

7 The Sundial
Just inside the main entrance is a sundial lined with zodiac signs. When commissioned in 1786, a ray of sunlight marked noon but it is no longer accurate because of changes in the Earth's rotation.

8 Cappella Jemale
The crypt beneath the main altar dates back to 1567, when Pellegrino Pellegrini

St Bartholomew Flayed statue

was appointed architect of the Veneranda Fabbrica. It was called the "confession" and was intended to be a choir for the canons and a place to protect martyrs', as well as saints', relics honoured by the Ambrosian Church.

9 Treasury

Located in the Duomo Museum, the treasury holds a fine and extensive collection of liturgical objects dating as far back as the 5th century.

Chalice from the Treasury

10 The Façade

The soaring Neo-Gothic frontage is punctuated with a riot of colourful stained-glass windows and five solid doors with bronze reliefs largely dating back to the 19th century.

THE CONSTRUCTION

Milan's Duomo is a massive construction worked on over six centuries by the best craftsmen and architects from all over Europe. Surprisingly the church was completed in a more or less homogenous style – Italy's only Gothic cathedral. The first stone was laid in 1386 by the Duke of Milan, Gian Galeazzo Visconti, as an offering for an heir. The medieval management company founded to oversee the project, the Veneranda Fabbrica del Duomo, is responsible for the cathedral to this day. Canals were constructed to transport building materials, including marble from quarries on Lake Maggiore. The high altar was consecrated in 1418 by Pope Martin V, but the façade was not completed until 1813, when Napoleon promised that the French treasury would fund its construction.

The opulent façade of the Duomo was completed in 1813 on orders from Napoleon, who was crowned King of Italy inside in 1805.

TOP 10 DUOMO FACTS

1 The fifth-largest cathedral in the world

2 There are 2,244 statues outside, mainly of saints but including one of Napoleon Bonaparte

3 11,700 sq m internal area

4 135 spires

5 96 gargoyles

6 1,100 statues inside

7 52 columns along the central nave (one for each week of the year)

8 158 m (518 ft) long

9 93 m (305 ft) wide at the widest point

10 108 m (354 ft) high

TOP 10 ⭐ Verona

Some 20 km (12 miles) east of Lake Garda, Verona is best known as the setting for Shakespeare's *Romeo and Juliet*, but it was also one of the main Roman towns in Northern Italy and flourished in its Renaissance heyday under the della Scala family. Verona has always been a prosperous place, and the town centre, nestling in a bend of the River Adige, is a rich patchwork of buildings from different eras.

1 Arena
Every summer Verona's Roman amphi-theatre **(above)** becomes the stage for epic productions of popular operas – Verdi's *Aida* is always included. The 15,000-seat arena has a wonderful atmosphere.

2 Duomo
This Romanesque-style cathedral, built in the 12th century, contains pilasters and beautiful frescoes in red Verona marble. Its structure was altered many times over the course of the centuries.

3 Torre dei Lamberti
Standing 84 m (276 ft) high in Piazza delle Erbe, this brick tower was built between 1172 and 1463. Take the lift or climb the 368 steps up to the top for views over the city.

4 Castelvecchio
The Castelvecchio **(below)** is a red-brick fortress with battlements that extend across the river on the fortified Ponte Scaligero bridge. Commissioned in 1354 by Cangrande II, it now holds a museum of sculpture and art.

5 Teatro Romano
This impressive Roman theatre was excavated in the 1800s and partly reconstructed. It is now a striking backdrop for concerts and shows.

6 San Fermo
This is two churches in one: Benedictines built a simple lower church to house the remains of saints Fermo and Rustico, while a splendid upper Gothic church was built by Franciscans for worship.

Verona

L. MATTEOTTI
Adige
VIA A FORTI
C. CAVOUR
VIA MAZZINI
VIA R CAPPELLO
PIAZZA BRA
VIA ROMA
Adige

1 km
(0.5 miles)

⑨ Sant'Anastasia
Verona's pink-hued marble softens the lines of the interior **(left)** of this Gothic church and acts as a backdrop for Pisanello's fresco *St George Preparing to Save the Maiden* in the chapel to the right of the altar.

ROMEO AND JULIET

Shakespeare's tale of star-crossed lovers was probably based on a novel published in 1530 by Luigi da Porto. There is little proof that the story is factual, although Verona was famous for feuding families, and records show Capuleti (Capulet) and Montecchi (Montague) families at the time of Bartolomeo I della Scala. Volunteers at the Juliet Club reply to letters from around the world that are addressed to Juliet.

⑩ Piazza delle Erbe
Once the site of the Roman Forum, then a market in the Middle Ages, this bustling square **(below)** is lined by civic institutions such as the Casa dei Mercanti and the Palazzo del Comune, plus various palaces.

⑦ Casa di Giulietta
This 13th-century palazzo was drawn out of anonymity with the addition of a balcony. Rubbing the right breast of the statue of Juliet in the courtyard will supposedly bring you a new lover.

⑧ San Zeno Maggiore
The façade of this church is centred by the "wheel-of-fortune" window and framed by a slender bell tower. Mantegna's striking *Madonna and Saints* adorns the altar.

NEED TO KNOW

MAP H4

Verona Tourist Office: Via Degli Alpini 9; 045 806 8680; open daily

Arena: Piazza Brà; open 8:30am–7:30pm daily (from 1:30pm Mon); €10

Duomo: open Mar–Oct: 10am–5:30pm Mon–Sat, 1:30–5:30pm Sun;

Nov–Feb: 11am–5pm Mon–Sat, 1:30–5:30pm Sun; €2.50

Torre dei Lamberti: Cortile Mercato Vecchio; 045 927 3027; by reservation only, call ahead to book; €6

Castelvecchio: Corso Castelvecchio 2; open 10am–6pm; €6

Teatro Romano: open 10am–6pm; €4.95

San Fermo: Opening times vary, check website; www.chieseverona.it/en/visit-info

Casa di Giulietta: Via Cappello 23; open 9am–7pm Tue–Sun; €6

San Zeno Maggiore: same hours as the Duomo; €3

Sant'Anastasia: Piazza Sant'Anastasia; open 10:30am–4:30pm Mon–Fri (to 6pm Sat), 1–5:30pm Sun; €3

TOP 10 ⭐ Centro Lago and its Villages

The point where the two branches of southern Lake Como meet is known as Centro Lago. Pretty lakeside towns and splendid villas with luxurious gardens enchant visitors. The lake water and surrounding mountains combine to create a temperate climate. Villages here include sleepy Varenna to the east, sporty Menaggio to the west and beautiful Bellagio, on the tip of the promontory.

Varenna
Enchanting Varenna **(right)** has villas with pretty gardens, a ruined castle and a maze of cobbled streets to explore. Its sleepy waterfront is the perfect spot to simply unwind.

2 Villa del Balbianello, Lenno
Perched on a lush wooded promontory on the western shore, the villa *(see p78)* has terraced gardens and grand rooms **(below)** offering breathtaking views over Isola Comacina and the centre of the lake.

3 Pescallo
Over the eastern side of the Bellagio promontory, this tiny fishing hamlet is a hidden delight. Sit in the shade and enjoy views of the lake from the waterside café.

NEED TO KNOW

MAP N2–N3

Varenna Tourist Office: Via IV Novembre 7; 0340 830 367; opening times vary, check website; www.varennaturismo.com

Villa del Balbianello: Via Comoedia; open mid-Mar–mid-Nov: Tue & Thu–Sun; €22; www.visitfai.it

Castello di Vezio, Varenna: Frazione Vezio, Perledo; opening times vary, check website; €5; www.castellodivezio.it

Villa Serbelloni, Bellagio: by guided tour only, check website for details; €10; www.villaserbelloni.com

Menaggio Tourist Office: Piazza Garibaldi 3;

0344 329 24; opening times vary, check website; www.menaggio.com

Villa Carlotta, Tremezzo: Via Regina 2; 0344 40405; check website for times; €10; www.villacarlotta.it

■ **La Punta (Punta Spartivento, Bellagio)** is a panoramic spot for a drink.

4 Shopping in Bellagio

Bellagio's stepped alleyways and main Via Garibaldi offer a host of goodies – from top-label clothes to jewellery and shoes. Local leather, wood and lacework are among the many other delights on offer.

Centro Lago and its Villages

LAKE FERRIES

Ferries, hydrofoils and cruises criss-cross the lake, with connections to all destinations. Fares are cheaper if bought before boarding; day passes are also available. Sailings become less frequent during low season. Information is available at booths at landing stages, tourist offices and online at www.navlaghi.it.

6 Villa Serbelloni, Bellagio

The lovely gardens at Villa Serbelloni are quieter than many and, while the terracing, grottoes and statuary equal its contemporaries, the views of the lake are unrivalled. The gardens (see p44) can be visited only on a guided tour.

7 Monte San Primo

Offering stunning views over Lake Como and the Alps beyond, Monte San Primo is a steep 3-hour hike from Bellagio along a well-kept track. The tourist office has route maps.

5 Castello di Vezio, Varenna

A short and steep 40-minute walk up the mountain behind Varenna takes you to the ruins of this 17th-century castle, with spectacular views, a pleasant café and falconry displays on weekends.

8 Menaggio

Near the Swiss border, Menaggio is the perfect base to enjoy Lake Como as well as the nearby golf course, hiking and cycle routes.

9 Villa Carlotta, Tremezzo

Best reached by boat to its own landing stage and then up the imposing scissored-staircase, the white Neo-Classical Villa Carlotta (see p79) features some of the finest gardens **(above)** on the lake.

10 San Giacomo, Bellagio

In the square at the top of Bellagio, the church of San Giacomo **(left)** is a wonderful example of local Romanesque architecture. The interior is rich with mosaics and home to a splendid 16th-century altar.

Bergamo

Nestled at the foot of the Alps, midway between lakes Como and Garda, this wealthy city has a long history. Conquerors, including Romans, Austrians and, most notably, the Venetians – who ruled for 300 years until the late 18th century – have left a mix of influences. The ancient upper town, Città Alta, is a warren of cobbled streets surrounded by impressive walls, while the lower town, Città Bassa, is a patchwork of 19th-century boulevards, imposing civic buildings and medieval lanes.

1 Teatro Sociale

Tucked away behind an often-closed door, this impressive three-tiered wooden theatre dating from 1807 had been unused since 1929. In 2009 restoration work was completed, and once again it hosts works of theatre.

4 Shopping

Pedestrianized Via XX Settembre in the lower town is the best place to head for clothes and shoe stores. The upper town also has a good selection of boutiques and gourmet delicatessens, although prices are not cheap.

Bergamo

2 Museo Donizettiano

Curio-lovers will be thrilled by the museum's collection of music scores, instruments and the personal effects of Bergamo's famous composer of melodramatic opera, Gaetano Donizetti (1797–1848) **(above)**.

5 The Rocca

The Scala del Condannato (Prisoner's Staircase) inside the Rocca leads to the Museum of History, with a well-presented collection of photographs, weapons and medals.

3 Santa Maria Maggiore and Cappella Colleoni

The fabulously over-the-top Baroque interiors of the church are a taster for the extravagant funerary chapel next door. The Renaissance excess of coloured marble holds the tombs of a Venetian mercenary and his 15-year-old daughter.

6 Funicular

Trundling up the steep hill in a little two-car funicular railway through the ornate gardens of the city's splendid villas is the perfect way to arrive in Città Alta.

7 Palazzo della Ragione

The medieval arcaded building dominating Piazza Vecchia dates back to the 1100s. The old courthouse is topped with a bas-relief of the symbol of Venice, St Mark's lion **(left)**.

ARLECCHINO

The popular improvised Commedia dell'Arte theatre originated in Italy in the 16th century. According to tradition, the character Arlecchino (Harlequin) – the nimble, quick-witted servant in love with Colombina – is said to be Bergamese. Usually dressed in bright motley, Arlecchino has always been enacted with the gruff Bergamo accent in Italy.

NEED TO KNOW

MAP D3

Bergamo Tourist Office: Piazzale Marconi, Città Bassa; Via Colleoni 4, Città Alta; open daily; www.visitbergamo.net

Teatro Sociale: Via Colleoni 4, Città Alta

Museo Donizettiano: Via Arena 9, Città Alta; open Tue–Sun; €3

Santa Maria Maggiore and Cappella Colleoni: Piazza del Duomo, Città Alta; open 9am–12:30pm & 2:30–6pm Mon–Sat (to 5:30pm in winter), 9am–1pm & 3–6pm Sun

The Rocca: Via Rocca, Città Alta; open Jun–Sep: 10am–1pm & 2:30–6pm Tue–Fri (to 7pm Sat & Sun); Oct–May: 10am–6pm Tue–Sun; €5

Funicular: Viale Vittorio Emanuele II, Città Bassa; Piazza Mercato delle Scarpe, Città Alta; open daily; single ticket €1.30, 1-day ticket €3.50 or 3-day ticket €7

GAMeC: Via San Tomaso 53, Città Bassa; 035 270 272; open Wed–Mon; €8; www.gamec.it

8 The Walls

The 16th-century walls **(above)** are dotted with imposing gateways. The leafy avenues tracing the fortifications offer glorious views over to the Alps.

9 GAMeC

Housed in a 15th-century convent, Bergamo's modern and contemporary art museum *(see p41)* hosts a prestigious permanent collection, alongside excellent temporary exhibitions.

10 Piazza Vecchia

Guarded by the 52-m- (170-ft-) high bell tower, this square **(below)** in the heart of the upper town is lined with restaurants, with a library at one end facing the impressive Palazzo della Ragione.

TOP 10 ⭐ Lake Iseo

One of the area's best-kept secrets, Lake Iseo shot to relative fame in the summer of 2016 with the Floating Piers art installation, which allowed people to literally walk across the water. The area is gradually being discovered, but it is still refreshingly unspoiled. The hills of Franciacorta, just south of the lake, are covered with vineyards and dotted with villages and historic wineries.

Torbiere del Sebino Nature Reserve ①

Follow the trails at this watery reserve **(right)**, or head to the bird-watching tower with binoculars (see p87).

② Piramidi di Zone

These rocky pinnacles with mushroom-shaped caps were formed over time by erosion. They are linked by an easy trail with views over the lake and the island of Loreto.

③ Wine-tasting in Franciacorta

Almost all Franciacorta wineries (see p58) offer tours and tastings. Fascinating and informative, these tours provide a behind-the-scenes insight into how one of Italy's most prestigious wines is produced **(left)**.

④ San Pietro in Lamosa

This Romanesque monastery marks the start of a scenic trail. Parts of the complex date from the 11th century, but the frescoes in the church (see p42) are from the 15th–16th centuries.

NEED TO KNOW

Torbiere del Sebino Nature Reserve: MAP E4; adm; www.torbieresebino.it

Franciacorta: MAP E4; www.franciacorta.net

San Pietro in Lamosa: MAP E4; Via Monastero 5, Provaglio d'Iseo; open Sat & Sun

Accademia Tadini: MAP F3; Via Tadini 40, Lovere; open Apr & Oct: 3–7pm Sat,

10am–noon & 3–7pm Sun; May–Sep: 3–7pm Tue–Sat, 10am–noon & 3–7pm Sun; €10; www.accademiatadini.it

Monte Isola Tourist Office: MAP F3; Via Peschiera; 030 982 5088; open Apr–Oct; www.visitmonteisola.it

Bike hire: Franciacorta Bike Tours: www.franciacorta biketour.com; Iseo Bike, Via per Rovato 26, Iseo; www. iseobike.com

Parco Nazionale delle Incisioni Rupestri, Capo di Ponte: **MAP F2**; open Mar–Oct: 8:30am–7pm Tue–Sun; Nov–Feb: 8:30am–4:30pm Tue–Sun (to 1:30pm Sun); €6; www. parcoincisioni.capodiponte. beniculturali.it

■ Take in the lake's eastern coast from a 20th-century train. Visit www.trenodei sapori.area3v.com.

Lake Iseo

30 km (19 miles)

7 Iseo

Bustling Iseo has graceful piazzas and a fine lakeside promenade. There's plenty of cafés and shops, and colourful markets each Tuesday and Friday, plus a vintage market on the first Sunday of each month.

BAGÒSS CHEESE

The people of these valleys have traditionally led the tough life of subsistence-level cattle farming. Typical produce of this region includes the hard, strong-tasting Bagòss cheese, made with partially skimmed cow's milk. After careful preparation by hand, the cheeses are put aside for three years to mature, during which time they are scraped, oiled and turned at regular intervals.

5 Pisogne

This appealing lakeside village *(see p87)* was the gateway to the Val Camonica, and its buildings and artistic heritage demonstrate its importance. The main piazza is a great place for relaxing at a pavement café.

8 Monte Isola

Take the ferry to Peschiera Maraglio to explore the fishing villages and footpaths of this peaceful traffic-free island *(see p85)*. The views from the Madonna della Ceriola sanctuary at 600 m (1,970 ft) are stunning *(see p42)*.

9 Cycling

Cycling through Franciacorta's vineyards or around the lake **(above)** allows visitors to enjoy the peaceful atmosphere of the area. There are good cycle paths for all levels.

10 Rock Art, Val Camonica

Extraordinary prehistoric rock carvings are dotted through the Val Camonica area, north of Lake Iseo. You can see them at the Parco Nazionale delle Incisioni Rupestri at Capo di Ponte *(see p85)*.

6 Lovere

With winding lanes and a marina, Lovere has lots to offer. Highlights include the waterfront Accademia Tadini **(above)**, with works by Canova and Bellini, and the Santa Maria in Valvendra basilica.

🔟⭐ Sirmione and Southern Lake Garda

The hills around southern Lake Garda are carpeted by olive groves and vineyards. This is the area's most popular lake, complete with Roman remains, medieval villages and Venetian fortresses. The blue waters backed by mountain peaks and the Mediterranean climate are bewitching. Poking into the lake, the tiny village of Sirmione is the main attraction here, with Roman ruins and its own natural spa.

Peschiera del Garda ①
This old military town **(right)** has imposing 16th-century Venetian walls. It is the main rail hub for the lake and close to the area's theme parks.

② Lido delle Bionde, Sirmione
On the eastern side of the peninsula, white slabs of rock lead into the clean waters of the lake. Here, the beach, or lido, offers the best place for a dip.

Sirmione and Southern Lake Garda

③ Bardolino
The attractive village of Bardolino (see p94), on the southeastern side of the lake, gave its name to the local red wine that accompanies the lake-fish *antipasti* so well. Try a glass or two in the many *cantine*, or bistros, here.

④ Santa Maria Maggiore, Sirmione
Down a lane at the southern end of the village is the 15th-century church of Santa Maria Maggiore with an arcaded portico that was built using recycled Roman masonry. Inside, there is one central nave.

⑤ Villa Romana, Desenzano
A short walk from Desenzano's harbour stands Villa Romana, the remains of a late Roman villa, once the hub of a large agricultural estate here. Look out for the beautiful mosaic floors.

⑥ Lazise
Lazise's **(left)** role as an important Venetian port is borne witness by the village's remaining walls and the porticoed customs house by the little port. These days it is quieter than many of the larger resorts.

8 Rocca Scaligera, Sirmione

The Rocca Scaligera, a 13th-century moated fort **(left)**, guards the land entrance to Sirmione with turrets and swallowtail battlements. Climb up the steps to the towers and enjoy the views across the lake.

SOUTHERN GARDA WINES

Among the great wines of this area are the fruity Bardolino reds from the southeastern corner of the lake. The southern end produces drinkable white Lugana, Garda Classico and Custoza vintages. White Soaves and red Valpolicella are made near the eastern shore. The southwest produces a light rosé.

10 Grotte di Catullo, Sirmione

Perched at the tip of the Sirmione promontory, the open-air ruins of a large 1st-century AD Roman villa **(below)** stand among olive trees and rosemary bushes. The links with the poet Catullus are unproven.

7 San Pietro in Mavino, Sirmione

This little Romanesque church was built reusing Roman blocks. The frescoes inside date from the 13th to 16th centuries.

9 Desenzano

Lake Garda's main town *(see p94)* is just off the A4 motorway. The attractive centre bustles with residents. The castle and old harbour are worth a visit.

NEED TO KNOW

MAP Q5–R5

Peschiera del Garda Tourist Office: Piazzale Betteloni 15, 045 223 7183; open Jun–Sep: 9am–7pm daily

Lido delle Bionde, Sirmione: Viale Gennari 28, Sirmione; opening times vary, check website; www. lidodellebionde.it

Santa Maria Maggiore, Sirmione: open 8:30am–7pm daily (Nov–Feb: to 4:30pm)

Villa Romana Desenzano: open 9am–7:30pm daily (Nov–mid-Mar: to 5pm); €4

Lazise Tourist Office: Via Porto Vecchio 5

San Pietro in Mavino: Via San Pietro in Mavino 19, Sirmione; open

8:30am–7pm daily (Nov–Feb: closes 4:30pm)

Rocca Scaligera, Sirmione: open 8:30am–7:30pm Tue–Sat (to 1:30pm Sun); €5

Grotte di Catullo, Sirmione: opening times vary, check website; €6; www.grottedi catullo.beniculturali.it

■ Try the restaurant at the Grifone hotel *(see p115)*.

The Top 10 of Everything

The imposing battlements of the
Rocca Scaligera, Sirmione

🔟 Moments in History

Painting showing the Lombard League defeating Emperor "Barbarossa"

1 1st Century AD: Lake Como Flourishes

In the 1st century AD, the peace established by the Roman emperor Augustus and his successors enabled Northern Italian communities to flourish. Large agricultural estates were established and holiday villas were built around the lakes by residents of Milan, Bergamo and Brescia.

2 AD 313: Edict of Milan

Emperor Constantine issued the Edict of Milan in AD 313, granting Christians freedom of worship. Milan became a centre of Christianity under its charismatic bishop, Ambrogio.

Statue of Emperor Constantine

3 AD 773: Charlemagne Declared King of the Franks and Lombards

With the fall of Rome, northern European tribes swept down and sacked the lands without leaders. The Lombards established themselves at Pavia but were defeated by the Frankish king, Charlemagne. His rule brought about stability and peace to Europe.

4 AD 1176: The Lombard League Defeats "Barbarossa"

After numerous attempts to conquer Northern Italy, Emperor Frederick I – or Barbarossa – was defeated by an alliance of city states including Milan, Como, Cremona, Mantua, Bergamo, Brescia and Verona.

5 11th–15th Centuries: Renaissance City-States

From the 11th century the power of the city-states in Northern Italy was unrivalled: the della Scala family ruled Verona and its territories; the Gonzagas ruled Mantua; the Visconti and later the Sforza ruled Milan; and Venice was a republican city-state. After 1454, Northern Italy was dominated by the Sforza and the Venetian Republic.

6 1559: The Spanish Grants the Duchy of Milan

Marking the beginning of over 300 years of foreign rule, Milan fell into the hands of the Spanish, who did little to solve the economic and social problems of this period.

7 1861: Vittorio Emanuele II Crowned King of Italy

In 1796, Napoleon took over Austrian-ruled Northern Italy and threatened to destroy the old order, but in 1815 the status quo was restored. The Lombards continued to fight against foreign rule for five decades. In 1859, the Battle of Solferino, led by Vittorio Emanuele II, ended Austrian occupation in Italy. Vittorio Emanuele II became the first king of a unified Italy in 1861.

8 1919: Italy Gains South Tyrol from Austria

The border region with Austria had been disputed since 1866. The modern-day areas of Alto-Adige and Trentino were ceded to Italy for their part in World War I.

9 1945: Mussolini's Capture

On 28 April 1945, Benito Mussolini and his mistress Claretta Petacci were executed by the Resistance in the village of Mezzegra on Lake Como. Their bodies were taken to Milan and strung up in Piazza Loreto.

A performance at the Milan Expo

10 2015: Milan Expo

Milan hosted its second World Expo in 2015, focusing on the theme "Feeding the Planet, Energy for Life". Many parts of the city were rebuilt and several sustainable buildings were designed, including the IRCCS Galeazzi Orthopedic Institute, the Human Technopole research center and the Milan State University.

TOP 10 ROMAN SITES

Ruins of Brescia's Roman Temple

1 Roman Temple, Brescia
MAP F4 ▪ Via dei Musei
A partly reconstructed temple, originally built in AD 73.

2 Fontana di Madonna, Verona
MAP H4 ▪ Piazza delle Erbe
A 14th-century fountain in Piazza delle Erbe topped by a Roman statue.

3 Villa Romana, Desenzano del Garda
A sweeping 4th-century AD villa (see pp34–5) on the shores of Lake Garda.

4 Grotte di Catullo, Sirmione
The remains of a large 1st-century AD domestic villa (see p35) on a promontory in Lake Garda.

5 Colonne di San Lorenzo, Milan
MAP V5
This is a series of 16 Corinthian columns dating back to the 2nd century AD.

6 Teatro Romano, Verona
Restored in the 19th century, this (see pp26–7) is now a venue for music and theatre again.

7 Ruins of the Imperial Palace, Milan
MAP U3 ▪ Via Brisa
The remains of Emperor Maximian's palace were unearthed by World War II bombing.

8 Winged Victory Statue, Brescia
Life-sized bronze statue of Winged Victory (see p40) found in the city's Roman temple.

9 Arena, Verona
Verona's Roman amphitheatre (see pp26–7) can seat 15,000 people.

10 Porta dei Leoni, Verona
MAP H4 ▪ Via Leoni
This was the main entrance to the city of Verona from the south in Republican Roman times.

Works of Art

1 Andrea Mantegna's Dead Christ

Whether it is the perspective of this painting *(see p99)* that pulls you in or the realism of the colouring, your eyes feel drawn to every wrinkle of the shroud. The sense of bereavement emanating from the work might stem from the fact that Mantegna's own son had recently died.

2 Rock Art, Capo di Ponte

Spread across both sides of the Val Camonica above Lake Iseo are more than 140,000 symbols and figures that were carved in the rock *(see pp32–3)* over a period of 8,000 years.

3 Leonardo da Vinci's The Last Supper

The restricted visits and filtered air create a rarefied atmosphere for this masterpiece *(see p23)*, which lives up to the hype. The indignance of the disciples and the serenity of Christ as he announces that he will be betrayed by one of them is spellbinding. Notice, too, humble details such as the knotted tablecloth and the metal plates reflecting those used by the monks in the refectory.

Da Vinci's *The Last Supper* fresco

4 Winged Victory, Brescia

Discovered in the Tempio Capitolino in 1826, this Roman statue has become the symbol of the city. It is believed that this figure was altered in the 2nd century AD from an older statue of Aphrodite. Visit the Museo di Santa Giulia in Brescia's Parco Archeologico to see *Winged Victory (see p87)*.

Winged Victory, Brescia's symbol

5 Masolino Frescoes, Castiglione Olona

MAP B3 ▪ 0331 858 903 ▪ Opening times vary, check website ▪ Adm ▪ www.museo collegiata.it

Masolino da Panicale was commissioned to decorate the baptistry in this village. The frescoes tell the story of John the Baptist with artful portraits.

6 Da Vinci's Portrait of a Musician

Believed by some to be a self-portrait, critics doubt that da Vinci finished this painting in the Pinacoteca Ambrosiana *(see p101)*.

7 Mark Wallinger's Via Dolorosa

On permanent display at Milan's Duomo *(see pp22–5)*, this video installation shows Zeffirelli's 1977 film *Jesus of Nazareth* in silence, with 90 per cent of the image blacked out.

Raphael's *Angel*, housed in Brescia

8 Raphael's Angel, Brescia

MAP F4 ▪ Santa Giulia, Via Musei 55 ▪ 030 297 7833 ▪ Open 10am–6pm Tue–Sun ▪ Adm ▪ www.bresciamusei.com

Painted when Raphael was just 17 for San Nicolà da Tolentino in Umbria in 1501, the retablo was damaged by an earthquake and cut up. This fragment was discovered for sale in Florence; another is on display in the Louvre; and a third in Naples.

9 GAMeC, Bergamo

This gallery *(see p31)* displays a permanent collection of modern and contemporary works by artists from Italy, as well as other countries, including Kandinsky, Boccioni, de Chirico, Morandi, Fontana, Manzù, Sironi, Hartung, Cattelan and Xhafa. Educational programs, conferences and performances are regularly organized. Guided tours are also available for visitors.

10 Caravaggio's St Francis in Meditation, Cremona

MAP E6 ▪ Museo Civico "Ala Ponzone", Via Ugolani Dati 4 ▪ 0372 407 770 ▪ Open 2–6pm Tue–Fri, 10am–6pm Sat & Sun ▪ Adm

The star painting at Cremona's Museo Civico has all the hallmarks of Caravaggio. The dark canvas shows the saint hunched over in thought.

TOP 10 PERIODS IN ART AND ARCHITECTURE

1 Prehistoric
Rock carvings document prehistoric society, its organization and beliefs.

2 Roman
Roman culture has survived in carvings, mosaics and inscriptions, as well as buildings such as temples and early Christian baptisteries.

3 Romanesque
Simple architecture, triangular façades and internal frescoes are classic elements of the early Romanesque style.

4 Gothic
Gothic art was focused in the decorations of churches built between the 12th and 14th centuries.

5 Renaissance
Renaissance artists portrayed realism in their art; architects sought symmetry and proportion based on Classical style.

6 Baroque
The elaborate Baroque style was used in the Counter-Reformation drive to educate society in Roman Catholicism.

7 Neo-Classical
The late 18th and early 19th centuries saw new civic architecture referencing the Classical Greek and Roman styles.

8 Romanticism
A 19th-century revisiting of historical movements, in particular the Medieval.

9 Liberty
Italy's version of the Art Nouveau movement that had its heyday between 1880 and 1920.

10 Futurist
This was an early 20th-century movement that focused on mechanization and movement; many of the main advocates of Futurism were killed in World War I.

Prehistoric rock carvings

🔟 Churches

① San Pietro in Mavino, Sirmione, Lake Garda

Sirmione's oldest church *(see p35)* stands among the olive trees near the Grotte di Catullo. It was first built in the 8th century during the Lombard era, then altered in 1320. There are some stunning medieval and Renaissance frescoes in the simple interior.

② Santa Maria Annunziata, Salò, Lake Garda

MAP Q4 ■ Vicolo Campanile 2, Salò

This imposing lakeside cathedral dates from the mid-15th century. Its unfinished façade belies the artistic treasures within. Highlights include an intricate gilded altarpiece and a pair of paintings by the 16th-century artist Romanino (Girolamo Romani).

Central aisle, Santa Maria Annunziata

③ Madonna della Ceriola, Monte Isola, Lake Iseo

Take a 2-hour uphill hike from Peschiera Maraglio (or catch the minibus to Cure for a shorter walk) to this church at the highest point of the island *(see p33)*. Built over the remains of a pagan temple, the current structure dates from the 16th century.

Vibrant frescoes in Sant'Abbondio

④ Sant'Abbondio, Como

Just outside the centre of Como, this church *(see pp18–19)*, formerly the city's cathedral, is worth seeking out. Built in the 11th century from locally quarried grey stone over the remains of a much earlier church, it has twin bell towers. The interior features a spectacular series of medieval frescoes.

⑤ Santa Maria della Neve, Pisogne, Lake Iseo

Much of the interior of this simple 15th-century church *(see p87)* is decorated with an exceptional cycle of frescoes painted by Romanino in 1532–4 depicting the Passion of Christ. The detail is stunning and includes scenes such as three men throwing dice to win Jesus's robes.

⑥ San Pietro in Lamosa, Franciacorta

Probably built over a pagan temple, this Romanesque monastery *(see p32)* overlooking the Torbiere del Sebino Nature Reserve features some admirable medieval and Renaissance frescoes, including one depicting St Anthony, St Benedict and St Peter. Art exhibitions are often held in the Sala Bettini, located below the church.

7 San Giorgio, Bagolino
MAP Q2 ■ www.bagolinoinfo.it

A striking sight at the top of the hillside village of Bagolino, this 17th-century church features a slender bell tower and an elegant façade with a colonnaded entrance. Inside are colourful frescoes and paintings that have been attributed to Tintoretto and Titian.

8 Duomo, Como
The striking combination of medieval, Renaissance and Gothic styles that makes Como's cathedral *(see p18)* so special is the result of building work that began in 1396 and didn't end until 1740, when the cupola designed by Filippo Juvarra was finally complete.

9 Abbazia di Piona, Colico, Lake Como
This medieval priory *(see p79)* has a lovely location on a peninsula on the lake's northeastern shore. The church, dedicated to St Nicholas, has a simple interior and has fine 13th-century cloisters. Remnants of a previous church built on the site are still standing nearby.

Lakeside Santa Caterina del Sasso

10 Santa Caterina del Sasso, Lake Maggiore
This hermitage *(see p74)* built into the rock on the eastern shore is one of Lake Maggiore's top sights. The church, built in 1585, incorporates a couple of older chapels and the 14th-century bell tower. There are frescoes throughout the complex.

TOP 10 CASTLES

One of the Castelli di Cannero

1 Castelli di Cannero, Lake Maggiore
MAP K2
The evocative ruins of two medieval castles perched on tiny islands.

2 Castello Scaligero, Malcesine, Lake Garda
Soak up awe-inspiring views from the castle's courtyards *(see p92)*.

3 Rocca Scaligera, Sirmione, Lake Garda
Sirmione's 13th-century castle *(see p35)* is unbelievably picturesque.

4 Castello di Arco, Arco, Lake Garda
MAP S2 ■ Open 10am–7pm daily (winter to 4pm) ■ Adm
This castle has wonderful frescoes.

5 Rocca, Riva del Garda, Lake Garda
MAP S2 ■ Open 10am–6pm daily ■ Adm
Surrounded by water, this medieval castle houses the MAG museum.

6 Rocca d'Anfo, Lake Idro
MAP Q3 ■ Guided tours only, book online ■ Adm ■ www.roccadanfo.eu
Built into the rocky hillside over the lake.

7 Castello Quistini, Franciacorta
A 16th-century castle *(see p86)* surrounded by a spectacular rose garden.

8 Rocca di Angera, Lake Maggiore
This castle *(see p70)* overlooking the lake houses a collection of majolica.

9 Castello Visconteo, Locarno, Lake Maggiore
MAP L1 ■ Open Apr–Oct: 10am–noon & 2–5pm Tue–Sun ■ Adm
A museum in this 14th-century castle features a collection of Roman glass.

10 Castello di Vezio, Perledo, Lake Como
This castle *(see pp28–9)* has a falconry, which houses birds of prey. It is also popular for stunning lake views.

TOP 10 Gardens

The Italianate gardens at Villa Taranto on Lake Maggiore

1 Villa Melzi
MAP N4 ■ Lungolario Marconi, Bellagio, Lake Como ■ 0339 4573 838 ■ Open Mar–Oct: 10am–6pm daily ■ Adm ■ www.giardinidivillamelzi.it

Villa Melzi was designed in the informal English style in 1808. The lawns stretch down to the water's edge with palms, cypresses and plane trees framing the wonderful views.

2 Isola Madre
Acquired in the 16th century from the diocese of Novara, Isola Madre *(see pp12–13)* was made first into a fruit orchard, then an olive grove and finally a citrus grove. Today, its botanical gardens are home to exotic flora, mature trees, shaded paths and fine views. French novelist Gustave Flaubert (1821–80) declared it to be his favourite island.

Luxuriant gardens on Isola Madre

3 Villa Taranto
Scottish sea captain Neil McEacharn created a botanical garden, complete with dahlias and azaleas, a bog garden, a huge pond with floating water lilies and an Italianate garden *(see p71)*. When he died in 1964, he was buried in a mausoleum in the grounds. Among the park's rare botanical species is the Victoria cruziana, a tropical water lily native to South America that produces enormous pads that can reach up to 2m (7 ft) in diameter.

4 Villa Serbelloni
Commonly speculated to be the site of Pliny the Younger's Roman villa, the villa gardens *(see p29)* are some of the quietest on the lakes. There are lovely views of the point where the three branches of Lake Como meet from the belvedere in the wooded upper garden. Near the house, the 18th-century formal section is split into curved terraces with topiary and statues.

5 Isole di Brissago
Just offshore in the Swiss section of Lake Maggiore, the tiny island of San Pancrazio, one of the Isole di Brissago *(see p15)*, was transformed into a splendid botanical garden in 1856 by the wealthy Baroness Antoinette de St Léger.

A staggering variety of species are on display, including Japanese banana trees, Chinese tea plants and shady Canarian palms.

6 Villa Carlotta

The gardens of Villa Carlotta, *(see p79)* on Lake Como, are a mix of terraces, statues, fountains and staircases. The spring flowering of 150 species of rhododendrons and azaleas is a splendid sight, as are the ancient cedars and sequoias. The Japanese-inspired bamboo garden with waterfalls is a soothing retreat.

7 Isola Bella

Created in the 1600s, Isola Bella *(see pp12–13)* is famed for the Baroque excesses of its terrace gardens, which contain a Roman theatre. Sprinkled everywhere are various stone structures, including stone stairs, obelisks and balustrades. White peacocks strut amid statues of angels, coiffured hedges and fragrant groves.

A reclining Buddha at Heller Garden

8 Heller Garden

This botanical garden *(see p95)* features flora from around the world, such as orchid meadows and giant ferns, while ponds with water lilies and lotus flowers are home to trout and carp. It has over 3,000 species of plants, and is dotted with sculptures, including statues from India and contemporary pieces.

9 Villa del Balbianello

The approach from the water is unforgettable, with steps leading up a scissor staircase, past statues and topiary to the pretty loggia *(see p28)*. The grounds are a delightful blend of flowery borders and geometrical hedges, plus huge trees.

10 Villa Cipressi

MAP N2 ■ Via IV Novembre 18, Varenna, Lake Como ■ 0341 830 113 ■ Open 7am–7pm daily ■ Adm

Named after the large cypress trees in the grounds, this villa stands at the top of the terraced garden that leads down to the water. It houses a hotel and a restaurant.

Manicured lawn at Isola Bella

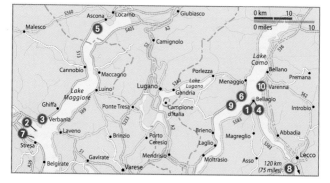

Walks

1 Val Cannobio, Lake Maggiore

MAP J2

This 7-km (4-mile) mountain route takes you through the Val Cannobio to Malesco. Take the bus from Cannobio town to the start point at Cursolo, and you can pick up the train at Malesco.

River Cannobio, Malesco

2 Centovalli, Lake Maggiore

You can pick up several trails from the stone hamlet of Verscio, a stop on the scenic Centovalli Railway (see p69) from Locarno. A woodland path leads for 4 km (2 miles) to Streccia.

3 Sacro Monte, Orta San Giulio

Short but steep mule tracks above Orta wind up through woodland to the 20 chapels of Sacro Monte (see p17). It is a great spot for a picnic.

Tableaux at Chapel XX in Sacro Monte

4 Monte Isola, Lake Iseo

Explore the circumference (9 km/5.5 miles) of the traffic-free island (see p33) by bike or on foot. Take a detour to the hilltop Santuario della Madonna della Ceriola for spectacular mountain and lake vistas.

5 Monte Baldo, Lake Garda

Hike on established trails to Monte Baldo, above the picturesque town of Malcesine. The cable car (see p55), which climbs to a height of 1,600 m (5,250 ft) in the first 10 minutes, can save you either the upward or downward journey, depending on how energetic you are feeling.

6 Brunate to Torno, Lake Como

The Como funicular (see pp18–19) whisks you up to the start of this walk in Brunate. Waymarked trails lead for 12 km (8 miles) to Torno, where you can see ancient tombs carved into the rocks. You can take the boat back to Como.

7 Argegno to Ossuccio, Lake Como

MAP M3

Start with a cable-car ride from Argegno up to Pigra. From here, you can walk for 12 km (8 miles) along old stone tracks through the Valle della Camoggia, and then via a Roman road to Ossuccio, which sits opposite Isola Comacina.

The Greenway del Lago di Como route

8 Greenway del Lago di Como, Lake Como

This very well-signed route follows cobbled paths and quiet lanes past the gardens of Villa del Balbianello (see p28) and Villa Carlotta (see p79). The total distance – from Colonno to Cadenabbia di Griante – is 11 km (7 miles), but it can also be covered in shorter sections.

9 The Lungolago – Riva del Garda to Torbole, Lake Garda

MAP S2

An easy 4-km (2-mile) walk linking two settlements at the north of Lake Garda, via beaches and parkland. This blustery corner of the lake is popular with windsurfers, so you will see plenty along the way.

10 Orrido di Sant'Anna, Lake Maggiore

MAP K2 ▪ Via Sant'Anna 30, Traffiume ▪ 0323 70682 ▪ **Restaurant: open noon–1:45pm & 7–9:45pm; closed Mon (except Jul & Aug)**

This trail (8 km/5 miles there and back) runs from Cannobio along the banks of a river, which widens to become surprisingly dramatic. At the end you reach the church of Sant'Anna, where the Sant'Anna restaurant is perched above a gorge.

CABLE CARS, FUNICULARS AND TRAINS

1 Como–Brunate funicular, Lake Como
Take the funicular from Como's wooden lakeside station to Brunate (see pp18–19).

2 Argegno–Pigra cable car, Lake Como
MAP M3 ▪ 031 821 344
Climb over 650 m (2,130 ft) in just 4 minutes for mountain walks (see p80).

3 Città Alta funicular, Bergamo
This is the best way to reach Bergamo's historic upper town (see pp30–31).

4 San Vigilio funicular, Bergamo
Take this funicular from the old town up to the village of San Vigilio (see p86).

5 Orselina–Cardada–Cimetta cable car and chairlift, Locarno
A red cable car (see p64) travels from Orselina up to Cardada, followed by a two-seater chairlift to Cimetta.

6 Laveno–Monte Sasso del Ferro cable car, Lake Maggiore
MAP K3 ▪ www.funiviedellago maggiore.it
There are views over the Alps and the lakes at this spot, a favourite with paragliders.

7 Centovalli Railway, Lake Maggiore
Cross the border into Switzerland and enjoy stunning scenery along the way (see p69).

8 Treno dei Sapori railway, Lake Iseo
Enjoy quality local food and wine from the comfort of this panoramic train (see p32).

9 Treno Blu railway, Lake Iseo
Historic steam or diesel trains (see p65) run along the lakeside.

10 Malcesine–Monte Baldo cable car, Lake Garda
These revolving pods (see p55) whisk walkers, skiers and paragliders up the mountain.

The Malcesine–Monte Baldo cable car

🔟 Cycling Routes

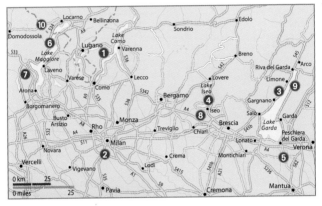

Cycling around Menaggio

1 Around Menaggio, Lake Como

One of the routes available from this section of the lake involves an ascent using the Argegno cable car to Pigra. From here you can climb up through alpine scenery along World War I defence lines to several mountain refuges with great views over lakes Como and Lugano. The trip down takes you along the old Menaggio–Porlezza train track. Contact the tourist office *(see p28)* for detailed information and cycle hire.

2 Along the Canals – Milan to the Certosa di Pavia

Head out through the southern suburbs of Milan along the towpaths towards Pavia *(see p101)*. You will cycle through villages, past bargemen's *osterie* (taverns) and beside rice fields for 20 km (12 miles) before you see the Carthusian monastery.

3 Gargnano to Limone via Tignale, Lake Garda
MAP R3

This is a challenging route of around 30 km (19 miles), taking in the steep slopes and winding side roads of the western side of Lake Garda. Just north of Gargnano, a narrow road climbs up to the village of Tignale (450 m/1,476 ft above the lake), offering splendid views. The road takes you higher still to Tremosine, from where it is downhill to Limone.

4 Around Monte Isola, Lake Iseo

A relaxed alternative to the strenuous ride up to the sanctuary at the top of the Monte *(see p33)* is the round-island trip of 9 km (6 miles). There are no private cars on the island, so the well-kept roads make for a pleasant ride. Refuel at one of the restaurants serving traditional Italian cuisine.

5 Mincio to Peschiera del Garda

MAP H6–G4 ▪ www.valeggio.com

This flat 43-km (27-mile) ride takes you through the Mantuan plains along quiet asphalted back roads from Mantua (Mantova in Italian) to the shores of Lake Garda. It is worth stopping off at Borghetto sul Mincio to try the local speciality, *nodo d'amore* tortellini, at one of the many restaurants. The Ponte Visconteo, the castles and the many water mills in the area are also worth a look before heading off along the Mincio to Peschiera.

6 Cannobio to Orrido di Sant'Anna, Lake Maggiore

There is a very pleasant ride inland from Cannobio on the northwestern shore of Lake Maggiore. An 8-km (5-mile) round-trip cycle path traces the river away from Cannobio beach through the countryside to the Orrido di Sant'Anna, a lovely gorge and a waterfall. There are places for picnics along the way, or the Ristorante Sant'Anna at the falls *(see p47)* is good, too.

7 Monte Mottarone, Lake Maggiore

MAP J3 ▪ Stresa ▪ 340 357 2189 ▪ www.bicico.it

If you're driving, two different routes will take you to the panoramic view-point of Monte Mottarone (1,491 m/ 4,892 ft) *(see p74)*. Bikes are available for hire at the base station or on the top of the mountain. Well-marked paths will bring you down.

8 Through the Franciacorta Vineyards

The timelessness of Franciacorta *(see p32)* makes it a wonderful place to explore by bike. Choose a route that lets you pop into a couple of the wine-growing estates, or enjoy a meal at one of the local restaurants.

Lakeside bike trail around Malcesine

9 Around Malcesine, Lake Garda

The tourist office at Malcesine *(see p92)* has put together six cycle routes based around the village. They cater to all levels, from a 90-minute trip through olive groves and along the lake to a 60-km (37-mile) freeride on Monte Baldo. Many utilize the town's cable car. The tourist office also has details of bike hire companies.

10 Through the Ossola Valley

MAP K1 ▪ www.vigezzina.com

Take the train to Camedo, then hire a bike and glide through the valleys along country lanes and over viaducts down to Pontebrolla, where you can pick up the train again.

Dramatic views and steep paths in the Ossola Valley

TOP 10 Swimming Spots

Shingle beach with mountain views at sunset, Torri del Benaco

1 Torri del Benaco Beach, Lake Garda

Located at the end of the promenade to the north of town, this beach *(see p94)* is a good spot for cooling down. Lake views have the Trento mountains as a backdrop and there is a leafy public park on the corner with a children's playground and a little café.

The beach at Sirmione, Lake Garda

2 Lido delle Bionde, Sirmione, Lake Garda

Halfway to the end of Sirmione's promontory a road leads off Via Catullo towards the town's lido *(see pp34–5)*. It is a good spot for swimming and sunbathing, and pedalos and canoes are available for hire. When in need of refreshment, there is a pizzeria and a café serving salads and sandwiches.

3 Manerba, Lake Garda
MAP Q5

Located on the western coast at the south of Lake Garda, Manerba is bordered with 11 km (7 miles) of fine beaches with fabulous views across the lake to the distant mountains. This is a flat area with many campsites that often have their own stretches for lakeside bathing, too. Manerba also has a lido with a pool and sunbathing areas.

4 Caneva The Aquapark, Lake Garda

Europe's largest water park at the southern end of the eastern shore of Lake Garda has something for each member of the family. There are slides and rapids, a relaxed beach and a sunbathing area, plus an exciting medley of children's theme sections, complete with pirate ships, an ancient lighthouse, a fishing village and an adventure island with an erupting volcano.

5 Belvedere, Iseo, Lake Iseo

MAP E4 ■ Via Rovato 28a, Iseo ■ 030 980 970 ■ Open late Apr–Sep: 9am–8pm Mon–Sat, 8am–8pm Sun ■ Adm ■ www.lidobelvedereiseo.it
This low-key lido on the edge of the town of Iseo has views across to Monte Isola. There are grassy sections and a shady picnic area, as well as a pool with slides and a beach. You can also hire canoes and pedalos.

6 Bellagio, Lake Como

If you cannot bear the heat, head towards the waters off the Punta Spartivento in Bellagio (see pp28–9). For more facilities, check with the tourist office whether the waterfront lido – on the way to Loppia – is open.

7 Punta San Vigilio, Lake Garda

MAP R4 ■ San Vigilio, Garda, Lake Garda ■ 045 725 5884 ■ Open Apr: 10am–6pm Sat & Sun; May: 10am–6pm daily (mid-May–end-May: to 7pm); Jun–early Sep: 9:30am–8pm daily ■ Adm ■ www.parcobaiadellesirene.it

In this charming little corner of the lake, the stony Parco Baia delle Sirene beach is backed by grassy olive groves. There's a picnic spot, kids' activities and refreshment kiosks.

Picturesque Punta San Vigilio

8 Cannobio, Lake Maggiore

Cannobio's beach (see p72) has been awarded an EU Blue Flag for cleanliness numerous times over the last few years. An attractive, spacious

The rocky beach at Cannobio

beach backed by shady trees, it offers various watersports such as wind-surfing and sailing, although it can get crowded in peak season. To get there, follow the lakefront road, Via Magistris, north out of the centre of Cannobio just past the car park at Piazza Martiri della Libertà.

9 Gravedona Beach and Lido, Lake Como

Just by the entrance into Gravedona towards the north of Lake Como is the town's beach and a small lido with two pools, a bar and great views over the lake and mountains (see p80). This is watersports territory, so there are many companies offering courses and equipment for hire.

10 Lido Giardino, Menaggio, Lake Como

MAP N2 ■ Via Roma 11, Menaggio, Lake Como ■ 339 321 3735 ■ Open Jun–early Sep: 8am–6pm daily ■ Adm

This complex on the northern outskirts of Menaggio offers a lake beach, some grassy patches, two pools, a children's playground and lovely sunbathing areas.

🔟 Outdoor Sports

Paragliding over the Lakes region

1 Paragliding

If you have a head for heights, floating off the sides of the mountains with great views over the waters is unmissable. Both tandem and solo paragliding descents are organized from Monte Baldo above Lake Garda (see p96) and Sasso del Ferro above Lake Maggiore, as well as at centres on the lakes in between.

2 Snowboarding

There are snowboarding pistes on the slopes around the lakes and the upper reaches of all the valleys. The ski resorts in the Val Camonica, Valli d'Ossola, Monte Baldo, Mottarone and around the north of Lake Garda are all good spots.

3 Hiking

All around the lakes there are marvellous opportunities for walking and hiking. Paths vary from mountain treks to strolls through olive groves. Suggestions for routes are available from local tourist offices, or you can put together your own with combinations of boats, cable cars and trains.

4 Kayaking

Paddling along the waters is the perfect way to get a closer view of the lakeside villas or to appreciate the soaring mountain peaks. Equipment can be hired on all the lakes, but it is most easily available at the northern end of lakes Garda and Como.

5 Horse Riding

Specialist companies arrange riding holidays in the area and tourist offices usually carry details of local companies. Some of the region's *agriturismi (see p113)* have riding facilities and some arrange treks.

6 Canyoning

The limestone gorges, waterfalls and glaciated features around the lakes are perfect for canyoning. This increasingly popular sport is available in numerous locations and there are various organizations in Torbole on Lake Garda, Stresa on Lake Maggiore and Grè on Lake Iseo.

7 Sailing and Windsurfing

Watersports are on offer all around the lakes but certain spots have ideal conditions and are particularly well regarded – especially around Torbole on Lake Garda (see p96), Pino on Lake Maggiore and the northern end of Lake Como around

Sailing – a popular pastime

Dervio. Even tiny Lake Iseo offers good facilities around Sarnico and Lovere (see p88).

8 Golf

MAP F4; Palazzo Arzaga, Brescia; 030 680 600 ▪ MAP M4; Circolo Golf Villa d'Este, Lake Como; 031 200 200 ▪ MAP N2; Menaggio & Cadenabbia, Menaggio, Lake Como; 0344 32103 ▪ MAP A4; Circolo Golf Bogogno, Bogogno, nr Lake Orta; 0322 864 137

There are several nine-hole courses around the lakes. The deluxe hotels in the area also offer some of the top courses in Europe, but fees are not cheap. Menaggio on Lake Como has the oldest course in the region.

Winter skiing high above the lakes

9 Skiing

Decent downhill and Nordic skiing opportunities are available at various locations above the lakes. Attractive pistes with equipment hire could keep you entertained for a few days, but the variety and length of runs do not compete with those located an hour or so further up in the Alps proper.

10 Mountain Biking

Practically every lakeside resort is within striking distance of somewhere with enjoyable mountain biking territory. Whether you prefer single-track cross-country rides or exhilarating downhill stints, there are routes throughout the region. Ferries and cable cars mean that you do not need to cover any territory twice.

TOP 10 SPECTATOR SPORTS AND RACES

The Giro d'Italia cycling race

1 Giro d'Italia
www.giroditalia.it
Watch the 100-year-old cycle race around Italy in May or June.

2 Marathon
milanocitymarathon.gazzetta.it
Milan's marathon, run through the centre of the city (mid-Apr), is one of the fastest in Italy.

3 Mille Miglia
www.1000miglia.eu
The exciting Brescia–Rome–Brescia vintage car race is held in May.

4 Centomiglia Regatta
www.centomiglia.it
Go to watch the 300 or more boats that race round Lake Garda in September.

5 Formula One
www.formula1.com
The Italian Grand Prix is held in September at a speedy track just outside Milan.

6 Rowing Races
These traditional races (Jun–Jul) pit local neighbourhoods against each other.

7 Palio Remiero del Lario
These rowing competitions (Aug) attract teams from across the region.

8 Football
www.legaseriea.it
Don't miss a game from the stands of the region's numerous top-league teams.

9 Windsurfing Competitions
Lake Garda attracts various international windsurfing competitions, such as the European championships.

10 Horse Racing
www.ippodromitrenno.it
The horse racing at Milan's hippodrome is a fun day out.

Children's Attractions

① Gardaland

Located in the southeastern corner of Lake Garda, Italy's largest theme park *(see p96)* offers a fun day out for most ages, with roller coasters, space rides, a log flume, an Egyptian area and zones for younger kids too. There are thrilling open-air shows, theatre performances and live entertainment throughout the day.

A fun ride at Gardaland theme park

② Pizza and Gelati
www.grom.it

Few kids turn their nose up at food they can eat with their hands. On pizzas, simple toppings like tomato and mozzarella should work for fussy eaters; the more adventurous can explore myriad other options. *Gelati artigianali* (homemade ice creams) fill the gaps between meals. A visit to GROM *gelateria* is a good way to experience tasty flavours.

③ Steamer Trip, Garda
MAP R4 ▪ Adm
▪ www.navlaghi.it

Steamboats are a great way to chug about Lake Garda. The summer-only service uses well-maintained boats dating from 1908. It has fewer sailings and destinations than other ferries but takes in most of the larger resorts.

④ Caneva The Aquapark, Garda
MAP R4 ▪ Via Fossalta 58, Lazise ▪ 045 696 9900 ▪ Open daily; check website for times ▪ Adm ▪ www.canevapark.it

Designed to resemble a Caribbean island with white sand and an erupting volcano, this aquapark has water slides and rides, shoots, jumps and rapids to keep the older children busy. A full-sized galleon, pirates and a water playground add to the fun. There are also calmer pools where you can relax and paddling pools for babies. Dining and shopping are also catered for.

⑤ Giardini Pubblici, Milan
MAP X1 ▪ Porta Venezia, Milan
▪ Metro Palestro, Turati & Porta Venezia

Play areas for different ages, a lake with carp and turtles, a merry-go-round and, at weekends, dodgem cars, pony rides and a miniature train, all fit into Milan's central park while still leaving space to kick a football or have a picnic in the shade.

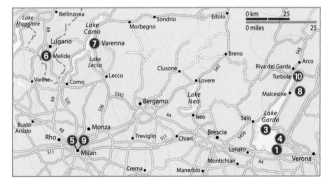

Strolling through the model village at Swissminiatur

6 Swissminiatur, Melide
MAP L3 ■ Melide 6815, Switzerland ■ (+41) 91 640 10 60 ■ Melide station ■ Open mid-Mar–end Oct: 9am–6pm daily ■ Adm ■ www.swissminiatur.ch

Backed by snow-covered mountains, this beautifully landscaped model village in Switzerland offers scale repro-ductions of over 100 Swiss buildings and Milan's Duomo.

7 Castello di Vezio
Perched at the top of the cliff with a great view over Lake Como, these castle ruins (see p29) are 40 minutes of steep steps up from the Varenna landing jetty. A good outdoor bar-restaurant, weekend falconry displays and a fossil exhibition add to the fun.

8 Cable Car, Monte Baldo
MAP S3 ■ Via Navene Vecchia 12, 37018, Malcesine ■ 045 740 0206 ■ Operates end Mar–mid-Nov: 8am–6:45pm daily ■ Adm ■ www.funiviedelbaldo.it

The revolving pods on Monte Baldo's cable car travel up the mountain from Malcesine, on the eastern shore of Lake Garda. There are dizzying views en route, and the top of the mountain offers hiking (see p46), mountain biking and paragliding opportunities.

9 Castello Sforzesco, Milan
Once drilling on the parade ground has been exhausted, the weaponry and armour in the castle museum (see p22) will keep some children entertained for hours; others might be taken by the slightly incongruous Egyptian collection.

Windsurfing at Torbole, on Lake Garda

10 Windsurfing, Torbole
www.torbole.com

Torbole on Lake Garda is a paradise for windsurfers. The calm waters of the mornings are perfect for novices; when the breezes stir up, there is enough to challenge anyone. Kite-boarding and sailing classes and equipment are also available.

🔟 Culinary Specialities

Polenta and roast vegetables

towns of Bergamo and Brescia and in their valleys. The pasta is usually freshly made as a starter and commonly served topped with melted butter and sage leaves (burro fuso) and a sprinkle of Grana Padano cheese.

① Polenta

This simple staple of corn meal or grits has nourished generations of northern Italians. Traditionally served up with donkey stew, veal or creamy cheese, it is cheap and filling. These days it is often left to cool, cut into slices and served up with lake fish or grilled vegetables.

② Cheeses

The area is strong on cheese-making. Mild or strong versions of blue-veined Gorgonzola and the semi-soft tangy Taleggio are widely available. The Monte Veronese cheeses are excellent, both mild and mature, and another less common cheese to try, on its own or with pasta, is the deep-yellow, well-structured Bagòss from Bagolino.

③ Lake Fish

Tinca (tench), *persico* (perch) and *luccio* (pike) are three of the most common lake fish on local menus. They are white fish with delicate flavours that are frequently offered simply grilled or baked, although they can be served in many other ways. *Missoltini* are small, sun-dried shad, pressed, salted and preserved in oil.

④ Casoncelli or Casonsei

Ravioli, or pasta parcels stuffed with sausage meat and cheese, are a speciality around the

⑤ Olive Oil

www.oliogarda dop.it/en

Thanks to its unusually mild microclimate, Lake Garda is a successful player in the world of Italian olive oil and benefits from European PDO (protected denomination of origin) status. The olives harvested each autumn produce a delicate oil that works well with the local lake-fish specialities.

⑥ Risotto

Northern Italy produces vast quantities of rice. As well as the classic *risotto alla milanese* – bright yellow thanks to the saffron it contains – many of the lakeside restaurants offer rice cooked with the area's most prestigious wine, Amarone, or served with perch fillets, tench or other lake fish.

Creamy risotto with mushrooms

7 Panettone and Pandoro

These tall, sweet breads are a must during the festive season throughout Italy. Light and yeasty, panettone hails from Milan and traditionally contains raisins and candied fruits; custom dictates that a slice should be eaten on 3 February to ward off colds. Golden *pandoro* from Verona is plain and slightly denser and comes dusted with icing sugar.

8 Pizzoccheri

This delicious vegetarian pasta dish originates in the Alpine area of Valtellina, just north of Lake Como. Strips of buckwheat pasta are served with a hearty combination of mild Valtellina Casera cheese, Parmesan, butter, cabbage or green beans, garlic and potatoes.

A classic *cotoletta alla Milanese*

9 Cotoletta alla Milanese

One of the most ubiquitous dishes on menus in Milan is *cotoletta alla Milanese*. Lightly breadcrumbed veal cutlets are fried in butter and served with a squeeze of lemon. There is usually nothing else on the plate, so if you want a side order, ask for vegetables or salad separately.

10 Cassoeûla

The classic way to beat the cold, foggy nights of a Milanese winter is to indulge in a heavy *cassoeûla*. This hearty pork and sausage casserole includes cabbage and variations of many other winter vegetables. A legacy of the Spanish occupation of the region in the 16th century, it is served at winter festivals and in restaurants that specialize in traditional Lombard cuisine.

TOP 10 RESTAURANTS FOR LOCAL DISHES

Simple elegance at La Streccia

1 La Streccia
Generous portions of local seasonal produce are served up with excellent homemade bread and pasta (see p75).

2 Ittiturismo da Abate
Run by fishermen, so the dishes couldn't be fresher. Try the pasta with lake-fish ragout or *missoltini* (see p81).

3 La Fagurida
A countryside trattoria offering tasty home-cooking, including asparagus in April and May (see p81).

4 Osteria al Bianchi
Hearty Brescian staples in a century-old *osteria* in the centre of town (see p89).

5 Trattoria Milanese
Traditional elegant dining rooms serving Milanese specialities including risotto and *cotoletta* (see p105).

6 Silvio
Fresh fish from Lake Como stars in dishes inspired by local culinary traditions (see p81).

7 Trattoria al Porto
Fried lake fish, perch fillets and ravioli with char and Bagòss cheese are among the specialities served here (see p89).

8 La Botte
Snug restaurant serving Piemontese country specials including game and wild mushrooms (see p75).

9 Il Cigno dei Martini
A smart restaurant in a 16th-century building in the heart of Mantua serving tasty local cuisine (see p105).

10 Al Bersagliere
Dishes include fish from nearby Lake Garda, Monte Veronese cheeses and risotto with Amarone (see p97).

Local Wines

1 Lugana
www.consorziolugana.it
Produced in a relatively small area around the southern end of Lake Garda, Lugana is made with a native white grape called Turbiana. With a fresh yet rounded character, it goes well with the local lake fish.

2 Chiaretto
Rosé wines are something of a rarity in Italy, but they're gaining in popularity, and some of the best are made around Lake Garda. Light and fruity Bardolino, Garda and Valtènesi versions of Chiaretto are available at the many lakeside wine bars.

3 Bardolino
www.ilbardolino.com
One of Lake Garda's best known and most historic red wines, Bardolino is made predominantly with native Corvina grapes, but it can include several other varieties. Local wineries have been working hard to raise the standards, with good results.

4 Custoza
www.cantinadicustoza.it
Produced around the southeastern shores of Lake Garda – between Lazise in the north and the enchanting village of Borghetto sul Mincio in the south – this is one of the area's most drinkable white wines. Sapid yet light and fresh, Custoza works well with the lake's fish dishes.

Wine cellar in the Soave area, Veneto

5 Soave
www.ilsoave.com
This versatile white wine comes from the medieval walled town of Soave, just east of Verona. While a simple Soave is best on its own, the Classico and Superiore varieties have more structure and work well with even complex dishes. Recioto di Soave, made with dried grapes, is ideal with strong-flavoured cheeses or desserts.

6 Franciacorta
Italy's most prestigious sparkling wine is produced just south of Lake Iseo (see p32). It's made according to the traditional method, similar to Champagne, and it comes in several varieties including Satèn, which has a soft, creamy effervescence, and Millesimato, from a single vintage and aged for three years. The characterful red and white Curtefranca wines are also made here.

Vineyards in Franciacorta

7 Valpolicella
www.valpolicellaweb.it

Wine has been made in this area since Roman times. The very name Valpolicella is thought to come from *valis polys cellae*, Latin for "land of many cellars". This red wine is made with three native varieties – Corvino, Rondinella and Molinara – and gains body in the *ripasso* version *(see p91)*.

8 Amarone
www.valpolicellaweb.it

Made in the same area and with the same grape varieties as Valpolicella, Amarone is one of Italy's main red wines. Dry, robust and harmonious, it retains its characteristics for 10–20 years. The wine-making process involves drying the grapes on racks for 100–120 days.

Bottles of Amarone wine

9 Garda Classico
www.stradadeivini.it

Garda Classico wines are produced to the west of Lake Garda. The reds are made mainly with the Gropello grape, which gives a spicy, fruity character; the fresh, fragrant whites are made with Riesling grapes.

10 Valtellina
www.stradavinivaltellina.com

This mountainous area north of Lake Como makes some excellent wines. The most common grape growing on the steep hillside terraces is Nebbiolo, used to make such characterful red wines as Sforzato, a robust, dry *passito*, and five different varieties of Valtellina Superiore – try the Grumello.

TOP 10 WINERIES AND WINE BARS

The Serego Alighieri winery

1 Serego Alighieri
Run by descendants of the poet Dante, this Valpolicella winery offers tours, tastings and is also a hotel *(see p117)*.

2 Tenuta Canova
Winery tours, a traditional trattoria and a multisensory wine museum *(see p97)*.

3 Il Cicheto
MAP R4 ▪ Via XX Settembre 33, Garda
Enjoy wines made nearby and bar snacks made with the daily catch.

4 Enoteca del Lugana
MAP R5 ▪ Viale Marconi 42, Sirmione
The place to buy some liquid souvenirs.

5 Vineria Rèfol
MAP S2 ▪ Piazza Alpini 8, Torbole
Buy local wines at this laid-back store or enjoy them here.

6 La Mandorla
MAP H4 ▪ Via Alberto Mario 23, Verona
This small wine bar near Verona's Arena serves good local wines.

7 Coffele
MAP H4 ▪ Via Roma 5, Soave (Verona)
An organic winery and one of Soave's best, Coffele has attractive cellars.

8 Cantine di Franciacorta
MAP E4 ▪ Via Iseo 98, Erbusco, Franciacorta
A one-stop shop stocking local wines.

9 Ca' del Bosco
MAP E4 ▪ Via Albano Zanella, 13, Erbusco ▪ www.cadelbosco.com
Book online for a tour and tasting at this exclusive Franciacorta winery.

10 Pronobis
MAP M4 ▪ Via Lambertenghi 19, Como
The wines to buy or drink here are selected from all over Italy.

🔟 Festivals

Colourful band entertaining the crowds during the Carnival festivities

① Carnival
Feb/Mar

The riotous celebrations before Lent involve dressing up and lots of mischief. Lecco, Bagolino and Verona are three places worth visiting to enjoy traditional processions.

② Clusone Jazz Festival
Jun

The medieval streets and Liberty summer houses of this town in the Valle Seriana host top international names at its established jazz festival.

③ Sagra di San Giovanni, Lake Como
The nearest Sat to 24 Jun

The Sagra di San Giovanni sees celebrations in the town of Como, with music and folk festivals culminating in a big firework display on the *notte di San Giovanni*.

Fireworks, Sagra di San Giovanni

④ Milan Gay Pride
End of Jun

For a whole week LGBTQ+ friendly events, such as parades, market stands, parties and shows are hosted in the streets around Via Lazzaretto, Via Lecco, Via Castaldi, and Largo Bellintani.

⑤ Festa del Lago, Varenna
First weekend of Jul

Boats arrive with "refugees" in medieval costume to commemorate Varenna taking in Isola Comacina's residents escaping Barbarossa in 1169 *(see p38)*. Then follows music, tasting sessions of local dishes and a spectacular display of fireworks.

⑥ Film Festival, Locarno
Early Aug ■ www.pardo.ch

This annual film festival is a hallmark of diversity and international talent. The 10-day event includes open-air screenings in the Piazza Grande with audiences of up to 8,000 people.

⑦ Music Festival di Stresa e del Lago Maggiore
Jul–Sep ■ www.stresafestival.eu

Since the 1960s this music festival has featured invited composers, orchestras, conductors and soloists.

The venues may include Santa Caterina del Sasso, the Basilica di San Giulio and the Isole Borromee.

8 Festa dell'uva, Bardolino
End of Sep/beginning of Oct
▪ www.bardolinotop.it

The grape harvest is celebrated in September throughout the region with wine, feasting and, often, song. In Bardolino, on the shores of Lake Garda, stalls are set up along the lakeside promenade serving hearty local food and wine. Various concerts are also organized.

9 Festa del Torrone, Cremona
Nov ▪ www.festadeltorrone cremona.it

Cremona sees itself as the home of *torrone*, or nougat, and celebrates the soft nutty concoction on the third and fourth weekends of November. Processions in medieval costume, dances and treasure hunts are features of this festival. There are also tasting sessions, children's cookery classes and a competition for the best recipe containing nougat.

Parade at Cremona's Festa del Torrone

10 Sant'Ambrogio, Milan
7 Dec

Milan's patron saint, St Ambrose, is celebrated with a large market near Sant'Ambrogio church. The day also marks the beginning of the opera season at La Scala *(see p22)*.

TOP 10 PUBLIC HOLIDAYS AROUND THE LAKES

Street entertainers on 25 April

1 1 January
New Year's Day, or *Primo dell'anno*.

2 6 January
Epiphany or *Epifania*. The day of the Befana, or good witch, brings presents to good children and coal to naughty ones.

3 Easter Monday
Known as *Pasquetta,* this is a popular day for picnics and visiting friends.

4 25 April
Liberation Day, or *Giorno della Liberazione*, celebrates the day when German forces left Italy at the end of World War II.

5 1 May
Labour Day, or *Festa dei Lavoratori*.

6 2 June
Republic Day, or *Festa della Repubblica*, commemorates the national referendum in 1946 when the people chose a republic instead of a monarchy.

7 15 August
The day of the Assumption of the Blessed Virgin Mary, known as *Ferragosto*, is celebrated in Italy by shutting up shop for the day.

8 1 November
All Souls' Day, or *Ognissanti*, is the day when people go to cemeteries to pay their respects to their deceased relatives.

9 8 December
The Feast of the Immaculate Conception of the Blessed Virgin Mary, or *Immacolata*, is celebrated on 8 December.

10 25 and 26 December
Christmas and Boxing Day are known as *Natale* and *Santo Stefano*.

TOP10 Italian Lakes for Free

1 Exploring Villages

Many lakeside villages have winding lanes and picturesque harbours overlooked by pavement cafés. Centuries-old churches often contain beautiful frescoes. Some of the best villages include Bellagio on Lake Como (see p29) and Cannobio on Lake Maggiore (see p72).

The village of Bellagio, on Lake Como

2 Villa Olmo, Como

A lakeside stroll from central Como takes you, past a number of lovely villas built by noble Milanese families, to this 18th-century villa (see p18). Its lovely gardens include a perfectly manicured Italianate section between the villa and the lake, and a romantic landscaped area behind.

3 Museums and archaeological sites

www.beniculturali.it

Every first Sunday of the month, Italy's state-run museums and archaeological sites have free entry, including such unmissable sights as the Grotte di Catullo and Rocca Scaligera in Sirmione (see p35), the Tempio Voltiano in Como (see p78) and the Val Camonica rock carving national park (see p85).

4 Villa Anelli Camellia Garden, Lake Maggiore

MAP K3 ▪ Via Vittorio Veneto 6, Oggebbio ▪ www.lacameliadoro.com

The climate at Lake Maggiore is perfect for camellias, and this idyllic garden is the place to see them. There are around 600 camellias of 450 different cultivars alongside other plants, many of them exotic.

5 Olive Oil Museum, Lake Garda

MAP R5 ▪ Via Peschiera 54, Cisano di Bardolino ▪ Open 9am–12:30pm & 2:30–7pm Mon–Sat, 9am–12:30pm Sun ▪ www.museum.it

This museum gives a real insight into the history of olive oil. Exhibits include huge wooden presses from times gone by, oil lamps and other paraphernalia. You can also watch a watermill in action.

6 Torre del Vescovo, Pisogne, Lake Iseo

This tower dominates the main piazza of the lakeside village of Pisogne (see p87). Built in the mid-13th century, it originally marked the lakeshore and was probably used for defensive purposes. Climb the 92 steps to the top for a striking, bird's-eye view of the area.

The Rocca Scaligera, in Sirmione

7 Bosco degli Gnomi, Zone, Lake Iseo

MAP F3 ▪ www.visitlakeiseo.info

Local artist Luigi Zatti, known as Il Rosso, continues his extraordinary undertaking to transform a stretch of woodland alongside the 227–227A footpath from Zone up to the peak of Monte Gugliemo into a magical "wood of the gnomes". His woodland sculptures include wolves, hares, bears and foxes, as well as gnomes.

8 Duomo, Como

Como's striking cathedral took nearly 350 years to build, and the changes in architectural styles only add to the harmonious effect of the whole. Among the decorations on the façade are statues of ancient Roman writers Pliny the Elder and Pliny the Younger, both born in Como (see p18).

The wine museum in Bardolino

9 Wine tasting and wine museum, Lake Garda

MAP R5 ▪ Cantina Fratelli Zeni, Via Costabella 9, Bardolino ▪ Open 9am–12:30pm & 2:30–7pm daily ▪ www.museodelvino.it

A free museum at this historic winery contains an interesting range of wine-making equipment. Visitors can taste most of the wines for free, apart from their most prestigious varieties. See the website for more details.

10 Walking

Walks – whether strolls along the waterfront or longer treks – are the best ways to enjoy the lakes (see pp46–7). Classic paths include the ancient Via Regina on the west coast of Lake Como and the Antica Valeriana from Pisogne to Pilzone on Lake Iseo

TOP 10 BUDGET TIPS

Charming Villa del Balbianello

1 National Trust members get discounts at Fondo Ambiente Italiano (FAI) sites, including at the Villa del Balbianello (see p28); RHS members can access Isola Bella free (see pp12–13).

2 The idyllic Parco Baia delle Sirene beach (see p51), on Lake Garda, reduces its entry fee in the afternoon and allows free admission from 6pm.

3 Multiday ferry passes, combined tickets for sights and family tickets all offer savings and are widely available.

4 Drinking coffee standing up at the counter is usually cheaper than sitting, since bars often charge for table service.

5 Service-charge percentages are sometimes listed in small print on restaurant menus in tourist areas; cover charges are normal, though.

6 Lunchtime sandwiches are generally cheaper, fresher and better quality from food stores and delis than from bars.

7 House wine, served by the quarter-, half- or full litre, is a cheaper alternative to buying a bottle.

8 Hotel fridges are ideal for keeping food and drink fresh, and room balconies (especially those with lake views) are perfect for a romantic picnic.

9 Hotels and campsites often offer free use of bicycles, a fun and no-cost way of getting around.

10 Carry an empty mineral water bottle with you, which you can then refill at public drinking fountains; the words acqua potabile mean the water is safe to drink.

🔟 Great Journeys

1 Lake Maggiore Express
This round-trip excursion includes a long ferry trip along Lake Maggiore, a scenic railway ride and a speedy train *(see pp14–15)*. The journey crosses into Switzerland, and you can start and end wherever you want on the lake and stop off as frequently as you like. Tickets are available all around the lake.

The Lake Maggiore Express railway

2 Brunate Funicular
This Art Deco funicular runs between Como and the hilltop village of Brunate *(see pp18–19)* in 30 minutes. Brunate is dotted with beautiful Liberty-style villas offering splendid panoramic views of the lake and beyond. It is the starting point for many treks around the lake, ranging from short two-hour walks to two-day hikes to Bellagio.

3 Locarno Cable Car and Chairlift
MAP L1 ■ (+41) 91 735 3030 ■ Adm ■ www.cardada.ch
Take the funicular railway up to the Santuario della Madonna del Sasso, above Locarno, then head for the cable cars that glide you up the incline to Cardada (1,350 m/4,429 ft). From here, there are awe-inspiring views across the peaks and lakes of the region. A 10-minute walk through the woods leads you to a chairlift to Cimetta (1,672 m/5,485 ft).

4 Boat to Isola Bella
Reaching Isola Bella by water from Baveno, Stresa or Verbania is unforgettable. As the Baroque terraces of the extravagant gardens *(see p45)* glide closer, the ferry circles the island to approach the landing stage, offering glimpses of secret corners of the gardens and palace.

5 Bergamo Funicular
This two-minute ride is the best introduction to Bergamo's Città Alta *(see pp30–31)*. The narrow train squeezes up from the lower town past 19th-century villas and through pretty gardens right to the heart of the medieval upper town.

Views from the Monte Baldo cable car

6 Monte Baldo Cable Car

State-of-the-art revolving cabins (see p55) offer panoramic views across Lake Garda as you rise up 1,760 m (5,775 ft) from Malcesine. Split into two sections, the route takes 20 minutes up to Monte Baldo, from where there are cycling and hiking routes galore as well as skiing and paragliding facilities.

7 Lakeside Walk from Lugano to Gandria
MAP L2–M2

Just outside Lugano (see p73), the little settlement of Castagnola is the start for the Sentiero di Gandria footpath. The path goes through the attractive Parco degli Ulivi to the appealing lakeside village of Gandria, 5 km (3 miles) away. The park extends up the hillside that becomes Monte Brè, and is lush with olive trees, cypresses, oleander bushes and scented shrubs.

8 Treno Blu
MAP E4 ▪ 030 740 2851
▪ Operates Mar–Oct ▪ www.ferrovieturistiche.it

Summer Sundays see this private train leave Palazzolo sull'Oglio for Lake Iseo, with occasional departures from Bergamo. At the lake, the train is met by a ferry that waltzes you around the lake with stopovers on the island of Monte Isola.

9 Cycling in the Mountains

In comparison with the crowded lakeside resorts and villages, the hills and mountains above the lakes in Northern Italy are generally little visited. Cyclists are spoiled for choice with mountain paths, rough tracks and winding roads (see pp48–9). Enjoy the views as you head down through vineyards, olive groves and lemon cultivations.

10 Lake Como Ferry
www.navlaghi.it

There are few better ways of enjoying the exquisite views of the lakeside villas and old fishing villages of Lake Como than from the ferry as it pulls in and out of the little harbours. The Centro Lago triangular trip takes in three of Lake Como's most delightful villages, chugging at a stately pace.

The Lake Como ferry picking up passengers from a small village harbour

Italian Lakes
Area by Area

**Busy market day on charming
Piazza delle Erbe, Verona**

TOP 10 Lake Maggiore and Around

A temperate climate has helped create the biggest draw of Lake Maggiore – its luxuriant gardens. From palm-tree lined promenades to the formal terraces of the Borromean Islands, Alpine gardens and the immaculate lawns of the Grand Hotels, Maggiore is in bloom throughout the year. The surrounding mountains and valleys offer myriad activities to complement lazy times by the lake. Just over Mount Mottarone, to the southwest, lie the tranquil waters of Lake Orta, the most westerly of the lakes.

Statue in Villa Taranto

LAKE MAGGIORE AND AROUND

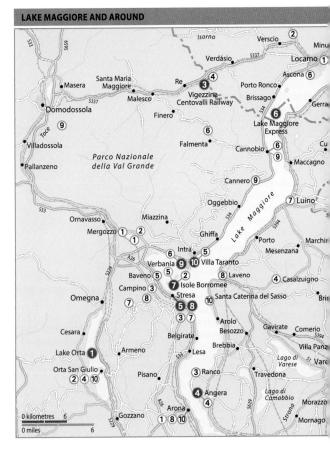

Elegant villas on tiny Lake Orta

① Lake Orta

Little Lake Orta *(see pp16–17)* is a serene backwater in comparison with its neighbours, although it too has been a tourist destination for several centuries. The northern tip is rather industrialized, but the southern end of the lake is hardly touched. Often referred to as the "pearl" of the lake, the village of Orta San Giulio, on the western shore, is one of the loveliest places in the region.

② Villa Panza

MAP L4 ▪ Piazza Litta 1, Varese ▪ 0332 283 960 ▪ Open 10am–6pm Tue–Sun; closed Jan ▪ Adm (free for National Trust members) ▪ www.fondoambiente.it

On the outskirts of Varese, Villa Panza features a collection of top-quality contemporary American art, including some site-specific installations from James Turrell and Dan Flavin. The works juxtapose beautifully with antique furniture and original decor.

③ Centovalli Railway

MAP K1 ▪ 0324 242 055 ▪ Adm ▪ www.vigezzinacentovalli.com

This scenic 52-km (32-mile) stretch of railway *(see p46)* between Domodossola in Italy and Locarno in Switzerland passes through craggy cliffs and wooded valleys, over vertiginous bridges and past half-forgotten villages, vineyards and waterfalls. You can break your journey as frequently as you wish to explore by bike or on foot.

A bridge on the Centovalli Railway

Vaulted interior, Rocca di Angera

④ Rocca di Angera
MAP J4 ▪ 0331 931 300
▪ **A walk uphill from Angera landing stage** ▪ **Open late Mar–mid-Oct: 9am–5:30pm daily** ▪ **Adm** ▪ **www.isoleborromee.it**

This medieval castle was bought from the Visconti by the current owners, the Borromeo family, in 1449. Wonderfully preserved, it enjoys a strategic position above the town of Angera, with extensive vistas across the southern reaches of the lake *(see p72)*. Highlights include the vaulted Sala di Giustizia (Law Court), decorated with 13th-century frescoes.

⑤ Golfo Borromeo
The bulge on Maggiore's western shore is home to the lake's best-known attractions. The popular resorts of Stresa and Baveno *(see p72)* face the Borromean Islands and, across the bay, Verbania. Watercraft shuttle from the shores to the islands, including the car ferry to Laveno on the eastern shore.

Baroque garden on Isola Bella, one of the Isole Borromee

FERRY SERVICE

Lake Maggiore is served by an efficient ferry service divided into four sections: the lower zone to Angera; the central zone including Stresa and Pallanza; the northern zone from Cannero to the border; and the Swiss basin. See www.navigazionelaghi.it for more details.

⑥ Lake Maggiore Express
This splendid trip combining ferry and rail through both Italy and Switzerland can take from six hours to a couple of days with as many stops as you like. Included are a boat trip on Lake Maggiore *(see pp14–15)*, the Centovalli Railway from Locarno to Domodossola and a train back to the lake.

⑦ Isole Borromee
Only three of the five tiny islands *(see pp12–13)* between Pallanza and Stresa are open to the public. Isola Bella, the most famous, is an extraordinary Baroque creation of palace, lakeside grottoes and formal gardens. On the island's narrow Vicolo del Fornello, fishermen's houses have been transformed into elegant boutiques selling Italian goods. Isola Madre is the largest island, but less ostentatious, with a modest villa and beautiful gardens. Isola dei Pescatori (or Superiore) houses a pretty fishing village, although it does not belong to the Borromeo family.

(8) Stresa

MAP J3 ▪ Tourist office:
Piazza Marconi 16, by the ferry jetty
▪ 0323 31308 ▪ Open 10am–2:30pm
& 3–6pm daily; end Oct–Mar: closed
Sat & Sun ▪ www.stresaturismo.it

Surrounded by the green slopes
of Mottarone, Stresa offers splendid views over the Borromean
Islands and the lake beyond. This
resort town was especially popular
with European aristocrats in the
1920s and 30s. Today, the waterfront Grand Hotels continue to
offer nostalgic grandeur.

Waterfront at Stresa, Lake Maggiore

(9) Verbania

MAP J3 ▪ Tourist Office: Via Ruga
44, Verbania Pallanza ▪ 0323 503 249
▪ Open 9:30am–12:30pm & 3–5pm
Mon–Sat ▪ www.verbania-turismo.it

Halfway up on the western side of the
lake, Verbania includes three adjacent
lakeside villages: Intra, Pallanza and
Suna. Intra is the transport hub for bus,
train and cross-lake ferries. Pallanza
is a low-key resort with a southerly
aspect and rare views across the lake.

(10) Villa Taranto

MAP J3 ▪ Verbania Pallanza
▪ 0323 404 555 ▪ Villa Taranto landing
stage ▪ Gardens: open Mar: 9am–
5:30pm daily; Apr–Sep: 9am–6:30pm
daily; Oct–Nov: 9am–4:30pm daily
▪ Adm ▪ www.villataranto.it

Captain Neil McEacharn bought this
villa in 1931 to fulfill his ambition of
creating a botanical garden (see p44).
The result is a mix of scents and col-
ours in flowering borders, woodlands,
greenhouses, and gardens with 300
types of dahlias and equatorial lily pads.

A DAY ON THE LAKE MAGGIORE EXPRESS

▶ MORNING

Boarding the **Lake Maggiore
Express** will mean a comfortable
start from the **Stresa** landing
stage with the 11:15am ferry
heading for **Locarno** (see p73).
You can have a leisurely three-
course lunch on board (book
before departure) as you pass
the landmarks of the lake.
Once past the **Isole Borromee**
the lake narrows round the
final squiggle and you pass
Cannero and **Cannobio** (see
p72) to the Swiss border.

LATE AFTERNOON

Past the **Isole di Brissago** (see
p15) at the northern tip of Lake
Maggiore, the elegant resort
of **Locarno** is an inviting place
to pass an hour or so. Wander
the cobbled alleyways off Piazza
Grande and relax with an ice
cream at one of the pretty pavement cafés before catching the
4:43pm train to Domodossola.

The breathtaking **Centovalli
Railway** (see p69) section of
the trip offers magnificent
panoramas as you pass through
mountain crevices and ancient
chestnut woods, and over gravity-
defying bridges before crossing
the border back into Italy and
arriving at the Italian town of
Domodossola an hour and a half
later. The town centre offers
various traditional trattoria if you
want an early dinner, or perhaps
just an *aperitivo* and a plateful of
nibbles from one of the bars with
outdoor seating. The last train
leaves Domodossola at 9:17pm
for the 21-minute trip to **Stresa**.

See map on pp68–9

Towns and Villages

Mergozzo
MAP J3
Around the 9th century, silt from the River Toce cut Mergozzo off from Lake Maggiore. Since then this sleepy village has fronted its own splash of water – tiny Lake Mergozzo (see p74).

Orta San Giulio
Enchanting Orta (see pp16–17) has stone buildings and a cobbled piazza with views across the lake of an islet and wooded hills beyond.

Ranco
MAP J4
Located on a headland, on the southeastern corner of Lake Maggiore, Ranco is a quiet place with an attractive waterfront. The area is home to many natural marvels, including a series of glacial boulders such as the Sasso Cavallazzo that lies on the shore of the lake.

The lush Ranco commune by the lake

Angera
MAP J4 ■ Tourist Office: Piazza della Vittoria ■ 0331 931 915
Opposite Arona, at the southern end of the lake, Angera is dominated by the medieval Rocca (see p70).

Baveno
MAP J3 ■ Tourist Office: Piazza della Chiesa 8 ■ 0323 924 632 ■ Open 9am–12:30pm & 3–6pm Mon–Sat; more restricted hours in winter
Baveno's tightly knit centre of lanes opens on to the lakeside with a delightful Art Nouveau landing stage.

Charming square in Cannobio

Cannobio
MAP K2 ■ www.procannobio.it
Surrounded by a mix of small hotels and campsites, this lovely low-key resort has a good beach (see p51) and a pretty village centre of steep lanes.

Luino
Popular for its Wednesday market (see p15), Luino is also the birthplace of Bernardino Luini – a follower of da Vinci. Luini's frescoes can be seen in the cemetery church.

Laveno
MAP K3 ■ www.vareseturismo.it
Lakeside Laveno is a useful transport hub and docking point for the regular cross-lake ferry to Intra on the western shore.

Cannero
MAP K2
This quiet resort enjoys a suntrap on the western shore, and is lush with citrus fruit and olive groves that add a touch of the Mediterranean.

Arona
MAP A3 ■ San Carlo: 0322 249 669 ■ Opening times vary, check website ■ Adm ■ www.statuasancarlo.it
The lake's most southerly town has a cobbled centre and good rail connections. Climb inside the 35-m- (115-ft-) high statue of San Carlo, just out of town, and peer out of his ears for dizzying views across the lake.

→ *See map on pp68–9*

Into Switzerland

 Locarno
Famous for its camellias and summer film festival, Locarno *(see p14)* has a grand arcaded central square where the whole town seems to congregate on summer evenings.

 Valle Maggia
MAP K1 ■ www.vallemaggia.ch
Just outside Locarno, Valle Maggia has a network of valleys leading up to unspoiled Alpine peaks.

3 Santa Maria degli Angeli, Monte Tamaro
MAP L2 ■ www.montetamaro.ch
At the top of the lake, gondolas rise up from Rivera to Monte Tamaro. Here, next to the top station with breathtaking views, stands Mario Botta's Santa Maria degli Angeli (1997), an intimate memorial chapel.

4 Centovalli Railway
This railway line *(see p69)* runs from Locarno in Switzerland, through narrow valleys and over ancient bridges to Domodossola in Italy. Also available as part of the Lake Maggiore Express *(see p70)*.

 Alto Ticino
MAP C1 ■ www.visit-moesano.ch
The Alto Ticino, a place of lonesome valleys and soaring skies, has two ancient passes – San Gottardo and San Bernardino – that linked north and south Europe in times past.

 Ascona
With its waterfront promenade looking out over the Isole Brissago, this is a popular resort *(see p14)* with German-speaking Swiss tourists.

7 Bellinzona
MAP M1 ■ Tourist Office: Piazza Collegiata 12 ■ (+41) 91 825 21 31 ■ Open 9am–6pm Mon–Fri, 9am–4pm Sat & Sun ■ www.bellinzonese-altoticino.ch
Low-key Bellinzona is home to fine architecture and a stupendous trio of UNESCO-recognized castles.

8 Lugano
MAP L2 ■ www.lugano-tourism.ch
This lively and chic city, the halfway point between lakes Maggiore and Como, sits proudly on its own lake.

9 Gandria
MAP M2
A romantic hideaway east along the lake from Lugano, Gandria tumbles down the hillside into the water. Terrace cafés offer idyllic views.

10 Monte Generoso
MAP M3 ■ www.montegeneroso.ch
Capolago on the southern shore of Lake Lugano is the access point for the rack railway up Monte Generoso (1,705 m/5,595 ft). The panorama takes in Milan and Turin, as well as lakes Como and Maggiore.

The San Bernardino pass, in the Alto Ticino

Beauty Spots

Lake Mergozzo's crystal-clear waters

1 Lake Mergozzo
This little lake *(see p72)* is connected to Lake Maggiore by a 2.7-km (1.5-mile) canal. It is ideal for a swim, and the lakeside village of the same name is enchanting.

2 Gardens of Isola Madre
The extensive gardens *(see p13)* with their pergolas of wisteria and ancient Kashmir cypress offer a tranquil retreat for this otherwise busy corner of the lake.

3 Stresa's Promenade
The manicured lawns of the Grand Hotels that line Stresa's *(see p71)* waterfront lead down to a palm-tree-lined promenade, or *lungolago*, with views of the small crafts buzzing between the Isole Borromee.

4 Villa della Porta Bozzolo, Casalzuigno
MAP K3 ▪ Casalzuigno ▪ 0332 624 136 ▪ Open Mar–Sep: 10am–6pm Wed–Sun; Oct, Nov & mid-Feb closes 5pm; closed Jan, early Feb & Dec ▪ Adm ▪ www.villabozzolo.it
This 16th-century country residence has immaculate landscaped grounds, complete with a lovely secret garden.

5 Villa Taranto
The villa *(see p71)* is closed to the public, but the gardens, with a maze made of dahlias and huge water lilies, are well worth a look.

6 Val Cannobio
Narrow roads wind up to green hillsides dotted with hamlets and working farms – a great area for hiking, trekking and cycling *(see p46)*.

7 Monte Mottarone
www.funiviadelmottarone.com
Drive or take a bus to the top of Monte Mottarone *(see p49)* for the views. There are footpaths and cycle routes, and ski facilities in winter.

8 Alpinia Botanic Garden
MAP J3 ▪ Viale Mottino 25, Stresa ▪ 0323 927 173 ▪ Open Apr–Oct: 9:30am–6pm daily ▪ Adm ▪ www.giardinobotanicoalpinia.altervista.org
Halfway up Mount Mottarone, above Stresa, these gardens offer splendid views across the lake to the Alps.

9 Val d'Ossola
www.distrettolaghi.it; www.parcovalgrande.it
This mountainous area stretches from Lake Maggiore to the Alps and includes the Val Grande national park, with its walking trails. Domodossola *(see p71)* is the area's main town.

10 Santa Caterina del Sasso
MAP K3 ▪ Opening times vary, check website ▪ www.eremosantacaterina.it
Set on a ridge 18 m (60 ft) above water and visible only from the lake, this monastery *(see p43)* offers lovely views.

Santa Caterina del Sasso monastery

Places to Eat

PRICE CATEGORIES

For a three-course meal for one, with half a bottle of wine (or equivalent meal), taxes and extra charges.

€ under €35   €€ €35–60   €€€ over €60

Enoteca Il Grappolo
MAP A3 ▪ Via Pertossi 7, Arona
▪ 0322 47735 ▪ Closed Tue ▪ €€

This wine bar and restaurant suggests wine pairings for each dish on the menu. The Piedmont beef dishes are excellent.

2 Piccolo Lago
MAP J3 ▪ Via Filippo Turati 87, Lake Mergozzo, Verbania ▪ 0323 586 792 ▪ Closed Mon & Tue ▪ €€€

Enjoy excellent innovative cuisine in a glass restaurant suspended over Lake Mergozzo.

3 La Rampolina
MAP J3 ▪ Via Someraro 13, Campino ▪ 0323 923 415 ▪ Closed Mon L ▪ €€

Just above Stresa, this popular restaurant has magnificent lake views from its terrace. The emphasis is on local ingredients: lake fish, cheese, and mushrooms from the nearby mountains.

4 Villa Crespi
MAP A3 ▪ Via Fava 18, Lake Orta, Orta San Giulio ▪ 0322 911 902 ▪ Closed Mon & Tue, Jan–Mar ▪ €€€

Michelin-starred restaurant, with cuisine combining Southern Italian flavours with local produce is beautifully presented here.

Elegant fare, Villa Crespi

5 Hotel Verbano
MAP J3 ▪ Via Ugo Ara 2, Isola dei Pescatori ▪ 0323 30408 ▪ Closed Nov–Mar ▪ €€€

Find a place on the waterside terrace after the crowds have left and tuck into delicious traditional local dishes.

6 Ristorante Milano
MAP J3 ▪ Corso Zanitello 2, Verbania ▪ 0323 556 816 ▪ Closed Tue ▪ €€€

One of the local top spots, with a menu of both sophisticated and simple dishes. Impressive wine list.

Lakeside setting of Ristorante Milano

7 La Botte
MAP J3 ▪ Via Mazzini 6, Stresa ▪ 0323 30462 ▪ Closed Wed ▪ €

A cosy *osteria* (see p57) with an alpine feel, offering hearty Piemontese cuisine: game, polenta and pasta.

8 Vecchia Arona
MAP A3 ▪ Lungolago Marconi 17, Arona ▪ 0322 242 469 ▪ Closed Wed ▪ €€

The menu here flaunts a mixture of traditional pasta dishes and some more unusual reinterpretations.

9 La Streccia
MAP K2 ▪ Via Merzagora 5, Cannobio ▪ 0323 70575 ▪ Closed Thu ▪ €€

Hidden away, this rustic trattoria (see p57) offers Piemontese fare – with mushrooms, meats and cheeses.

10 Pan & Vino
MAP J4 ▪ Piazza Motta 37, Orta San Guilio ▪ 393 858 3293 ▪ Closed Wed ▪ €

A pleasant deli with outdoor seating and a menu that offers platters of cold meat and cheese, with local wines.

See map on pp68–9

🔟 Lake Como and Around

The third-largest, and the deepest, of all the Italian lakes, Lake Como is 50 km (30 miles) long and 4.5 km (3 miles) across at its widest point, with its southern section divided into two branches. The lake is named after its main town at the southernmost tip but it is also known locally as Lario. Visitors have been flocking to these waters for centuries. In Roman times, both Pliny the Elder and the Younger had houses here and, since the 1700s, European aristocracy and industrialists have lined the shores with their villas. At the end of the 19th century, the Grand Tour encouraged elegant hotels, and these days the lake attracts a mixture of Italians and foreigners, holiday-makers and glitterati.

Villa del Balbianello

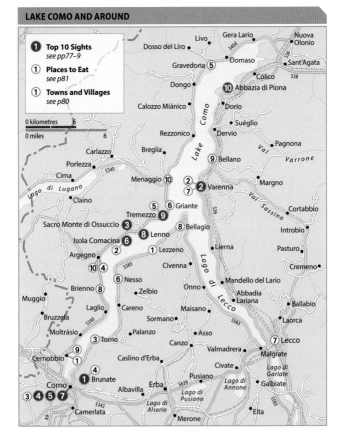

LAKE COMO AND AROUND

① **Top 10 Sights**
see pp77–9

① **Places to Eat**
see p81

① **Towns and Villages**
see p80

0 kilometres   6
0 miles   6

1 Brunate

A short ride on the funicular, or a steep uphill trek from Como, takes you to the charming village of Brunate *(see pp18–19)*. Here, Liberty villas rub shoulders with mountain-style homes, and there are unique views over the city and lake, as well as some good traditional restaurants and cafés. Brunate is the starting point for numerous walks and hikes that are signposted from the funicular station, including the path (a 30-minute walk) to the Volta Lighthouse, a monument erected to mark the centenary of Alessandro Volta's death.

2 Villa Monastero, Varenna

MAP N2 ▪ Via Polvani 2 ▪ 0341 295 450 ▪ May–Aug: 9:30am–7:30pm daily; check website for other months ▪ Adm ▪ www.villamonastero.eu

As the name readily suggests, Villa Monastero was built on the site of a former monastery. Rebuilt as a holiday retreat in the 16th century, these days it is used as a popular conference centre. The gardens have an astounding collection of plant species, and are dotted with several fountains, statues and temples. The villa has unrivalled views looking towards Pescallo on the Bellagio peninsula *(see pp28–9)*.

Lush corner of Villa Monastero

Tableau at Sacro Monte di Ossuccio

3 Sacro Monte di Ossuccio

MAP N3 ▪ Ossuccio ▪ 0344 55277

Nestling among olive groves with great views over the waters, this is one of nine UNESCO World Heritage *Sacri Monti* (Sacred Mountains) in Northern Italy. A world away from the crowds, the series of 14 chapels leading up to the sanctuary tells Bible stories with tableaux of life-size wooden statues. It is presumed that 17th-century Franciscan monks created the site to educate locals in teachings of what is now called Catholicism rather than the Protestant Reformation ideas sweeping the region at the time.

COMO CELEBRITIES

Lake Como has always attracted the rich and famous, including George Clooney, owner of Villa Oleandra in Laglio. Villa d'Este has hosted royalty, presidents and stars like Madonna. Villa Balbianello saw the filming of some iconic movies.

4 Silk Museum, Como

MAP M4 ▪ **Via Castelnuovo 9**
▪ **Open 2–6pm Tue–Sun** ▪ **Adm**

In the 16th century, Como became a world centre for silk. Today, raw silk is imported, but the production of fabric and the creative part is still carried out locally *(see p19)*. This museum shows how the industry developed.

Baroque interior of Como's Duomo

5 Duomo, Como

This attractive cathedral *(see p18)* is the happy result of changes in artistic styles in the 300 odd years it took for it to be completed. Its lofty dimensions and soaring arches are Medieval Gothic, the apses and tapestries inside are Renaissance and the 18th-century cupola is wonderfully Baroque. Dozens of colourful stained-glass windows brighten up the otherwise gloomy interior of the church; the oldest dates from the 15th century. Look out for the small frog carved in 1507 to the left of the north door, the Door of the Frog.

6 Isola Comacina

MAP N3 ▪ **031 821 955; 335 707 4122** ▪ **Boat from Sala Comacina: 9am–7pm daily; return ticket €7 (7pm until the end of service at the Locanda restaurant *(see p81)* return ticket €6)** ▪ **www.isola-comacina.it**

Isola Comacina, the only island on the lake, has a significant history. It was a pre-Roman settlement, a refuge for local warring factions in the Middle Ages and, finally, sacked by soldiers from Como in 1169. San Giovanni is the only standing church here but there are the ruins of at least five more.

7 Como Town

MAP M4 ▪ **Tempio Voltiano, Viale Marconi; open 10am–6pm Tue–Sun**

Como has a lively waterfront location and an attractive centre, with pedestrianized piazzas dotted with bars and restaurants and plenty of historic sites to visit *(see pp18–19)*. Locally born electricity pioneer Alessandro Volta is celebrated at the waterside Tempio Voltiano, as well as with a contemporary sculpture, *Life Electric*, at the end of the nearby pier.

8 Villa del Balbianello, Lenno

This 18th-century lakeside villa *(see p28)* holds the collections of the last owner, Guido Monzino, the first Italian to climb Everest. Scenes from *Star Wars Episode II* (2000) and *Casino Royale* (2006) were filmed here.

Lakeside Villa del Balbianello

Terraced gardens at Villa Carlotta

9 Villa Carlotta, Tremezzo

This 16th-century Neo-Classical villa *(see pp28–9)* flaunts paintings by Francesco Hayez (1791–1882), including the iconic *The Last Kiss of Romeo and Juliet*. The sweeping terraced gardens leading down to the waterfront are lush with a blaze of azaleas in spring, as well as banks of camellias and ancient cedars and sequoias.

10 Abbazia di Piona

MAP N2 ▪ Colico ▪ 0341 940 331 ▪ Ferry to Olgiasca ▪ Open 9am–noon & 2:30–6pm daily ▪ www.abbaziadipiona.it

On a peninsula on the upper reaches of the eastern shores of Como, this 12th-century priory sits on the site of a 7th-century church. The peaceful cloisters are the centre of the complex and the stone columns found here are covered with detailed carvings. The monks who look after the place make and sell a potent herb liqueur.

A DAY ON LAKE COMO

▶ MORNING

Start the day by exploring central **Como**, dedicating enough time to the **Duomo**. Wander the town's pretty cobbled streets and soak up the atmosphere from one of the many pavement cafés. Next, head down to the jetty to catch the ferry to **Bellagio** *(see pp28–9)*. After a spot of window-shopping around the picturesque lanes of the village, stroll down to the Punta Spartivento viewpoint for a panorama that encompasses all three branches of the lake. Enjoy a bite of lunch on the veranda at La Punta.

AFTERNOON

Back in Bellagio, sit down for an espresso or cappuccino at the historic Bar Rossi, with its wooden furnishings, then take the next ferry across the water to **Villa Carlotta**. Have a quick look at the 19th-century interior of the villa itself, then wander at will through the heady and luxuriant gardens and relax over a drink at the Antica Serra café, in the grounds, before heading back to **Como**. If it's a clear evening, take the funicular from the picturesque lakeside station up the hill to **Brunate** *(see pp18–19)* and admire the bird's-eye view over Como and the lake at sunset. Then take a table on the wisteria-canopied terrace of **Del Cacciatore** *(see p81)* and tuck into a hearty dish of polenta. If you're not staying in the village, remember that the last funicular down to Como leaves at 10:30pm from Sunday to Friday and midnight on Saturdays and in summer.

See map on p76 ←

Towns and Villages

1 Cernobbio
MAP M4

Just beyond Como, at the foot of Monte Bisbino (1,325 m/4,347 ft), this small town is most famous as the home of the Grand Hotel and gardens of the Villa d'Este *(see p114)*.

2 Varenna

Half asleep in the warm afternoon sun, Varenna *(see p28)* is the main attraction on the western shore of Lake Como, even though it is a low-key village with just a handful of sights and hotels.

3 Torno
MAP M4

A charming village on the eastern shore, Torno has terraced walkways and a pretty harbour overlooked by the Romanesque church of San Giovanni.

4 Argegno
MAP M3

The small town of Argegno gives the first glimpse of the impressive mountain ranges to the northeast and, with a quick zip up neighbouring Pigra (900 m/2,950 ft) in the cable car, there are even more breath-taking views of the lake.

5 Gravedona
MAP N1 ▪ www.gravedona.it

The main town in northern Lake Como, Gravedona is home to the lovely 12th-century church Santa Maria del Tiglio.

Panoramic view over Gravedona

6 Nesso
MAP N3

Down below road level, halfway between Como and Bellagio, the pretty stone village of Nesso is divided by one of the many gorges in this area and crossed by a delightful Roman humpbacked bridge.

7 Lecco
MAP P4 ▪ Tourist Office: Piazza XX Settembre 23 ▪ 0341 295 720 ▪ www.provincia.lecco.it/turismo

At the foot of the eastern fork of Lake Como, the small town of Lecco is the birthplace of 19th-century author Alessandro Manzoni.

8 Brienno
MAP M3

Tucked away from the main road on the western shore, this hamlet has narrow walkways weaving between the houses where the lake water laps up against the ancient stone.

9 Bellano
MAP N2

Bustling Bellano is a world away from the sleepy resorts further south. A spectacular gorge, or *orrido*, with metal walkways over the roaring river is the main draw.

10 Menaggio

Plump in the middle of the western shore of the lake, and on all the major ferry routes, Menaggio *(see p29)* is a great base for exploring the area.

Places to Eat

1 Ittiturismo da Abate
MAP N3 ▪ Frazione Villa 4, **Lezzeno** ▪ 031 914 986 ▪ Closed Mon ▪ €

Run by three brothers, this place *(see p57)* has a charming interior, a cheerful vibe and unbeatable fare.

Veranda, Locanda dell'Isola Comacina

2 Locanda dell'Isola Comacina
MAP N3 ▪ Isola Comacina ▪ 0344 55083 ▪ Open mid–Mar–Jun & Oct: Wed–Mon; Jul–Sep: daily; closed end Oct–mid-Mar ▪ €€€

The set menu here hasn't changed since 1947, and the meal is rounded off with a "fire ceremony".

3 Feel
MAP M4 ▪ Via Armando Diaz 54, Como ▪ 334 726 4545 ▪ Closed Sun ▪ €€€

The talented young chef serves gourmet dishes with a creative twist, including excellent pasta carbonara made with lake fish.

4 Del Cacciatore
MAP M4 ▪ Via Manzoni 22, **Brunate** ▪ 031 220 012 ▪ Closed Sun D & Mon ▪ €

Take the funicular to this trattoria with a wood-panelled interior and a shady veranda. Try the polenta with venison, gorgonzola or mushrooms.

PRICE CATEGORIES

For a three-course meal for one, with half a bottle of wine (or equivalent meal), taxes and extra charges.

€ under €35   €€ €35–60   €€€ over €60

5 La Fagurida
MAP N3 ▪ Via Rogaro 17, Tremezzo, Tramezzina ▪ 0344 40 676 ▪ Closed Mon ▪ €€

Specialities at this trattoria *(see p57)* in a stone farm building with lake views include polenta and fish.

6 La Cucina della Marianna
MAP N3 ▪ Via Regina 57, Cadenabbia di Griante ▪ 034 443 111 ▪ Closed Mon ▪ €€

Home cooking is on offer at this family-run *albergo-ristorante*.

7 Vecchia Varenna
MAP N2 ▪ Contrada Scoscesa 10, Varenna ▪ 0341 830 793 ▪ Closed Dec–mid-Feb; Mon & Tue during low season ▪ €€

Sit at a table virtually over the lake and enjoy game and good versions of the local fish dishes.

8 Silvio
MAP N3 ▪ Via Paolo Carcano 12, Bellagio ▪ 031 950 322 ▪ Closed mid-Nov–mid-Mar ▪ €€

A terrace with lake views complements the fish-based menu *(see p57)*.

9 Osteria del Beuc
MAP M4 ▪ Via Cavallotti 1, Cernobbio ▪ 031 341 633 ▪ Closed Mon ▪ €€

Dishes at this popular restaurant with simple decor include lake fish and buckwheat ravioli with *bresaola*.

10 La P'Osteria
MAP M3 ▪ Via Lungo Telo Sinistra 3, Argegno ▪ 031 447 4072 ▪ Closed Tue & Wed, Jan ▪ €€

This former post office serves Piemontese meats and lake dishes.

See map on p76

🔟 Bergamo, Brescia and Lake Iseo

Bergamo stands northeast of Milan at the foothills of the Alps guarding Northern Italy's main east–west roads and railway links. A prosperous place, Bergamo is best known for its attractive upper town, perched atop a hill. Lake Iseo, 20 km (12 miles) away, is one

of the prettiest of the smaller lakes in the region, with the glacier valley of Val Camonica stretching up to Switzerland behind. Bergamo's closest rival in local industry, football and just about everything else is Brescia, 43 km (27 miles) south-east. The relationship between the two towns has never been easy, but for a visitor the experiences are very different, with Brescia's Roman heritage complementing Bergamo's medieval splendours.

Mosaic in one of Brescia's Roman sites

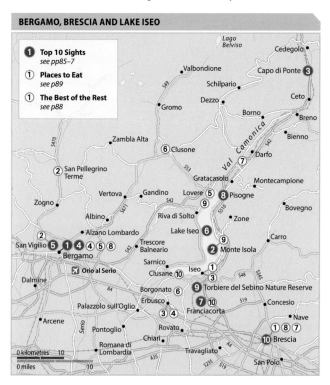

BERGAMO, BRESCIA AND LAKE ISEO

1 **Top 10 Sights**
see pp85–7

1 **Places to Eat**
see p89

1 **The Best of the Rest**
see p88

Previous pages The Isole Borromee on Lake Maggiore

One of the canvases on display at the Accademia Carrara, Bergamo

① Accademia Carrara, Bergamo

MAP D3 ▪ Piazza Carrara 82 ▪ 035 399 677 ▪ Open May–Nov: 10am–7pm daily; Dec–Apr: 9:30am–5:30pm Wed–Mon ▪ Adm ▪ www.lacarrara.it

Bergamo's main art gallery is based on the private collection of Giacomo Carrara, a merchant collector who bequeathed it to the city at the end of the 18th century. Masterpieces include works by Botticelli, Pisanello, Bellini, Lorenzo Lotto and Velázquez.

② Monte Isola, Lake Iseo

www.navigazionelagoiseo.it; www.tuttomonteisola.it

Rising up out of the middle of Lake Iseo, Monte Isola is the largest lake island in Europe (see p33) and was declared one of Italy's most beautiful boroughs in 2003. A wooded plug of rock, 3 km (2 miles) long and 600 m (1,970 ft) high, it has 12 hamlets and villages and is topped by the Sanctuary of Madonna della Ceriola. Bike hire is available and there are good paths for walking or cycling. It is a popular day trip and lunch spot with restaurants dotted along the shoreline, and a handful of B&Bs and hotels.

③ Rock Art, Capo di Ponte

The Val Camonica, north of Lake Iseo (see pp32–3), is littered with prehistoric rock carvings spanning several thousand years. Recognized as a UNESCO World Heritage Site, the Parco Nazionale delle Incisioni Rupestri (National Rock Carving Park; follow the yellow signs from the main road) is an open-air site with carvings recording local life over several millennia of civilization up to the Bronze Age. Stick figures show religious ceremonies, agricultural work, jewellery and even a cart and a blacksmith.

④ Upper Town, Bergamo

Take the funicular up to Bergamo's Città Alta, or upper town (see pp30–31), to see such remarkable buildings as the basilica of Santa Maria Maggiore, with its extravagant Baroque interior, and the adjacent Cappella Colleoni, a Renaissance masterpiece. The central Piazza Vecchia is the hub of everyday life, with many bars, a charming 18th-century fountain and a medieval bell tower. Head up the Campanone for spectacular views of the city and beyond. Stay for the evening, and you'll hear the bell ring 100 times at 10pm, originally a signal to citizens that the city gates were about to be closed.

Santa Maria Maggiore, Bergamo

Cruising on Lake Iseo is a leisurely way of exploring this region

5 San Vigilio, Bergamo
MAP D3

The tiny neighbourhood of San Vigilio, at the very top of Bergamo's upper town, has always been a half-forgotten corner of the city. At the beginning of the 20th century, a funicular was opened to attract day trippers to the neighbourhood. Little has since changed. There are a few restaurants and a bar and spectacular views across elaborate gardens. The ruins of the castle here have been turned into a pretty park with subterranean Venetian defence tunnels to be explored.

6 Cruises, Lake Iseo
www.barcaiolimonteisola.it; www.navigazionelagoiseo.it

To complement the regular ferry service around Lake Iseo, there are a number of round-the-lake cruises that run in the summer months. Typically, the cruises circumnavigate Monte Isola and the two tiny private islands on the lake – San Paolo and Loreto. Other options involve taking in the higher or the lower reaches of the lake. There is even a nighttime cruise with dinner on board.

7 Franciacorta
Castello Quistini: Opening times vary, check website; adm; www.castelloquistini.com

The wines made in the Franciacorta (see p32) hills have been highly regarded since ancient times (see p58). With wineries and hillside villages, Franciacorta has several monasteries, such as San Pietro in Lamosa (see p32), and castles such as Castello Quistini, famous for its rose garden. A great way to explore the area is by hiring a bike and cycling among the vines.

Bergamo as seen from San Vigilio

TRENO BLU

On some Sundays in summer, a privately run train (see p65) leaves Bergamo station for the scenic trip to Paratico, on Lake Iseo. Boats connect here to take you over to Iseo and the panoramic Monte Isola. Details are available from tourist offices or at www.ferrovieturistiche.it.

⑧ Pisogne

MAP F3 ■ Torre del Vescovo: open 10am–9pm Tue–Sun ■ Santa Maria della Neve: open 10am–6pm Tue–Sun

This lakeside village is dominated by the Torre del Vescovo tower, with superb views from the top. Pisogne's main draw, however, is the series of frescoes painted by Renaissance artist Romanino at the Santa Maria della Neve church, just outside the centre.

⑨ Torbiere del Sebino Nature Reserve

Footpaths and boardwalks encircle this expanse of water linking Lake Iseo (see p32) and Franciacorta. In June, water lilies light up the reserve's surface, but Torbiere is a lovely place for a walk at any time of year.

Torbiere del Sebino Nature Reserve

⑩ Parco Archeologico, Brescia

MAP F4 ■ Parco Archeologico & Museo di Santa Giulia: open 10am–6pm Tue–Sun; adm; www.brescia musei.com

Located near the Alps, the modern-day town of Brescia (Brixia) played a key role during the Roman rule. The Parco Archeologico features impressive ruins such as those of the Capitolium temple, a part-excavated theatre and the Santuario Repubblicano, with its wonderful frescoes and mosaic floors. The 1st-century monastery of Santa Giulia, now the Museo della Città, displays *Winged Victory*, a bronze statue of Aphrodite dating back to AD 73.

HALF A DAY IN CITTÀ ALTA, BERGAMO

▶ **MORNING**

Grab a table in the sun in **Piazza Vecchia** (see p85) for a late breakfast or morning coffee and simply take in the splendour of the square. The main sights of the city are a stone's throw away behind the Palazzo della Ragione, in **Piazza Duomo**. After your fill of Baroque exuberance in Santa Maria Maggiore and the Cappella Colleoni, if you have a head for heights, climb up the Campanone for panoramic views and ear-splitting chimes. From the square, bear left along **Via Colleoni** towards the **Cittadella**, perhaps popping into the **Teatro Sociale**, at No. 4, or any of the boutiques or delicatessens that line the route. Dive down any of the cobbled lanes that take your fancy; it will be easy to make your way back.

AFTERNOON

Just off Colle Aperto, through **Porta San'Alessandro** on the right, is the funicular up to **San Vigilio**; make sure you have change for a ticket from the machine. At the top, wander along the road in either direction for sweeping views over Bergamo and the plains. Visit the park in the old **castle ruins** for a little shade and a rest stop. The fresh wood-oven pizzas and delicious local dishes at **San Vigilio** (see p89) are an excellent choice for lunch. Take in the lovely views over the valley, stop for a photo and plan a route to walk down through **Porta San Giacomo** to the lower town.

See map on p84 ←

The Best of the Rest

Brescia Castle
MAP F4 ■ Via Castello 9, Brescia ■ Open 10am–6pm Tue–Sun ■ Adm

At this imposing fortress on Cidneo Hill, an easy stroll from the city centre, you can climb the towers and visit the arms museum.

The tower of Brescia Castle

2 San Pellegrino Terme
MAP D3 ■ Spa: open May–Sep ■ www.qcterme.com/en/san-pellegrino/qc-terme-san-pellegrino

This spa town, north of Bergamo, has a sprinkling of Art Nouveau buildings and lush gardens.

3 Iseo Town
MAP E4

Drop by the local produce market here on Tuesday or Friday mornings.

Teatro Sociale, Bergamo
This oval wooden theatre (see p30) hosts all manner of performances from drama to music.

5 Museo Donizettiano, Bergamo
The composer Gaetano Donizetti, born in Bergamo in 1797, is best known for his *Lucia di Lammermoor*. This museum (see p30) displays original letters and scores.

6 Clusone, Val Seriana
MAP E3 ■ www.turismo proclusone.it

This little town dotted with Liberty villas has a pretty medieval centre.

7 Val Camonica
MAP F3 ■ www.turismovallecamonica.it

Dotted with prehistoric rock carvings (see p85), the valley offers opportunities for hiking in summer and skiing in winter.

Pinacoteca Tosio Martinengo
MAP F4 ■ Piazza Moretto 1, 25121 Brescia ■ 030 297 7833/4 ■ Open 10am–6pm Tue–Sun

This brilliant art museum has works from the 13th to the 18th centuries in 25 exhibition show-rooms. Paintings on display include masterpieces by Raphael, Thorvaldsen, Hayes and several Renaissance Brescian painters such as Romanino and Moretto.

Watersports, Lake Iseo
MAP E3 ■ Sportaction, Solto Collina, Grè, Iseo ■ 340 984 3097; 0364 536 254 ■ www.monticolo.it; www.sportaction.it

Enjoy canoeing, windsurfing and sailing at many centres on the lake, including Gré, just south of Lovere.

Franciacorta Wine Region
Famous for its sparkling wine, vineyards and restaurants, this area (see p32) is dotted with picturesque villages, tranquil monasteries and patrician villas.

Vineyards in the Franciacorta region

Places to Eat

PRICE CATEGORIES

For a three-course meal for one, with half
a bottle of wine (or equivalent meal),
taxes and extra charges.

€ under €35 €€ €35–60 €€€ over €60

1 Ca' de Cindri
MAP E4 ▪ Via Duomo 46, Iseo
▪ 030 982 1543 ▪ Closed Tue ▪ €

Grilled lamb chops and lake-fish
specialities vie for pride of place
on the menu at this traditional
restaurant in Iseo. The homemade
pasta and desserts are tasty, too.

2 San Vigilio
MAP D3 ▪ Via San Vigilio 34,
Bergamo ▪ 035 253 188 ▪ €€

Delicious pizzas are served bubbling
from the wood-burning stove at San
Vigilio. Enjoy a slice along with lovely
views from the balcony.

3 La Smorfia
MAP E4 ▪ Via Costa 9, Erbusco
▪ 030 726 8434 ▪ Closed Tue ▪ €

Specialities at this simple, friendly
place in Franciacorta include a
monthly spit roast. Pizzas and
gourmet burgers are also served.
There's an excellent wine list.

4 Leonefelice Vista Lago
MAP E4 ▪ Via Vittorio Emanuele
23, Erbusco ▪ 030 776 0550 ▪ €€€

The views over Lake Iseo are
superb from the terrace of this
bistro at L'Albereta hotel (see p114).
Come for Sunday brunch for
a varied choice of hot and cold
dishes and Franciacorta wines.

5 Osteria Spirito Divino
MAP F3 ▪ Via del Cantiere
17, 24065 Lovere ▪ 035 983 861
▪ Closed Mon ▪ €€€

A minimalist interior and gorgeous
lake views define this elegant
restaurant. It specializes in fish
dishes with a creative twist
but several vegetarian options
are also available.

6 Due Colombe
MAP E4 ▪ Via Foresti 13,
Borgonato, Corte Franca ▪ 030 982
8227 ▪ Closed Mon ▪ €€€

Set in the heart of Franciacorta, this
Michelin-starred restaurant serves
wonderfully creative dishes that make
use of local seasonal ingredients.

7 Osteria al Bianchi
MAP F4 ▪ Via Gasparo da Salò
32, Brescia ▪ 030 292 328 ▪ Closed
Tue & Wed ▪ €

Traditional Brescian staples including
malfatti (spinach and ricotta dump-
lings) are served in this old-world
osteria (see p57), as well as plenty
of dishes from the rest of Italy.

8 Vineria Cozzi
MAP D3 ▪ Via Colleoni 22, Città
Alta, Bergamo ▪ 035 238 836 ▪ €€

This refined but friendly place offers
gourmet food and a superb selection
of local and national vintages.

Well-stocked bar at Vineria Cozzi

9 Locanda al Lago
MAP F3 ▪ Via Carzano 38,
25050 Monte Isola ▪ 030 988 6472
▪ Closed Tue ▪ €€

Take a table over the water and tuck
into lasagne with lake fish.

10 Trattoria al Porto
MAP E4 ▪ Porto dei Pescatori
12, Clusane sul Lago ▪ 030 989 014
▪ Closed Wed ▪ €

Try the prawn spaghetti at this
trattoria (see p57).

See map on p84

TOP 10 Lake Garda and Around

Lake Garda is an area of contrasts. The northern section is more rugged, with deep water and strong winds that make this part of the lake ideal for watersports. To the south, the edges of the lake are gentler, with stony beaches and vine-covered hills with lemon and olive groves. Garda is the largest of the main Italian lakes, measuring about 51 km (31 miles) in length. The water is the cleanest and the temperature far milder and more Mediterranean in nature than it should be for its latitude. This adds up to make Lake Garda the most visited of the Italian lakes; the waterside roads and villages can get jammed in season, but further afield there are idyllic valleys to explore as well as the appealing historic town of Verona.

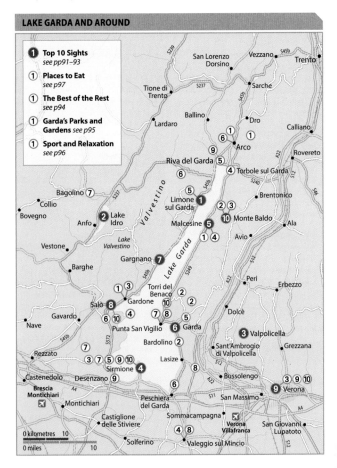

LAKE GARDA AND AROUND

1 **Top 10 Sights**
see pp91–93

1 **Places to Eat**
see p97

1 **The Best of the Rest**
see p94

1 **Garda's Parks and Gardens** see p95

1 **Sport and Relaxation**
see p96

0 kilometres   10
0 miles   10

The marina at Limone sul Garda

1 Limone sul Garda
MAP S2 ▪ Tourist Office:
Via 4 Novembre 29L ▪ 0365 954 720
▪ www.visitlimonesulgarda.com

Until the 1930s, Limone, on a narrow strip of land at the northwestern end of the lake, was only reachable by boat. It survived on fishing and olive and citrus fruit production. There is one *lemonaia* (lemon frame) left in the town as a reminder of its livelihood through the centuries.

2 Lake Idro
MAP Q3 ▪ Tourist Office: Via
Trento 27, Idro ▪ 0365 832 24 ▪ www.
lagodidro.it ▪ www.bagolinoinfo.it

Head west from Gargnano to reach Lake Idro, driving through the mountainous Valvestino area and passing tiny artificial Lake Valvestino on the way. Lake Idro makes a refreshing and peaceful contrast to Garda. It's surrounded by steep wooded hillsides and has its own share of pretty villages,

campsites and beaches with watersports facilities. The real highlight of the area, however, is the medieval village of Bagolino, famous for producing the tasty cheese Bagòss.

3 Valpolicella
MAP S5 ▪ Villa Mosconi
Bertani: www.mosconi
bertani.it ▪ Villa Rizzardi:
www.villarizzardi.it;
www.valpolicellaweb.it

This wine-making area, which lies between Lake Garda and Verona, is made up of a series of villages, noble villas and historic wineries, with row upon row of vines. The stone-built hillside village of San Giorgio, with its graceful Romanesque church, is particularly appealing. Villas to visit include Villa Mosconi Bertani and Villa Rizzardi, both featuring exceptional gardens. Serego Alighieri is a winery *(see p59)* organizing tours and tastings.

4 Sirmione
Jutting out from the southern lakeshore on a little promontory, Sirmione *(see pp34–5)* is a pretty, historical town perfect for day trips, although it is extremely busy in summer. The natural spa here, originating from the Boiola spring, made this a popular spot in Roman times. The town's main sight is the impressive Rocca Scaligera, a medieval castle dating back to the 13th century.

Roman ruins by the lake at Sirmione

5 Malcesine

MAP S3 ▪ Tourist Office: Via Gardesana 238; 0457 400 044 ▪ www.tourism.verona.it ▪ Castello Scaligero: open 9am–7:15pm daily; adm

Malcesine, on the eastern shore of Lake Garda, has cobbled lanes, a tiny harbour and a castle. In high season, the streets are full of visitors exploring the 13th-century Castello Scaligero (where Goethe was imprisoned for spying in 1786) or queueing for the cable car up Monte Baldo (see p55).

Malcesine's Castello Scaligero

6 Garda

MAP R4 ▪ Tourist Office: Piazza Donatori di Sangue 1, Garda ▪ 045 725 5824

A pleasant resort town built around a small bay, Garda has a long beach and a café-lined lakeside promenade. A tight network of lanes is set back from the water. There are some ancient stone buildings as well as shops selling souvenirs and leather goods. On the other side of the main road, villas, hotels and guesthouses stretch up the winding hillside.

7 Gargnano

MAP R3 ▪ Tourist Office: Piazza Boldini 2 ▪ 0365 791 243 ▪ www.gardalombardia.com

There is nothing much in this village except a pair of tiny harbours, a church and some waterside houses, but the atmosphere is delightful. DH Lawrence wrote *Twilight in Italy* here in 1912, and Mussolini stayed in the Villa Feltrinelli to the north of town for the last few months of his Salò Republic. Every September, the crowds pour in for the Centomiglia Regatta sailing race (see p53).

8 Salò

MAP Q4 ▪ Tourist Office: Piazza San Antonio 4 ▪ 0365 21423 ▪ www.gardalombardia.com

Salò is a bustling town on the western shore of the lake. The streets leading back from the waterfront are excellent for shopping, and the Renaissance Duomo rewards a brief visit. Elegant old *palazzi* line the streets, while sleek yachts bob in the large marina. Salò famously gave its name to Mussolini's Repubblica di Salò, a puppet regime set up for his last 18 months in power.

LAKE FERRIES

Lake Garda can be visited at a relaxed pace aboard ferries, hydrofoils and catamarans. There are also car ferries crossing the lake between Toscolano-Maderno and Torri del Benaco. Details are available at landing stages, tourist offices, and by calling 800 551 801. Visit www.navlaghi.it for timetables.

Opera production at Verona's Arena

9 Verona
Opera festival: www.arena.it

Best known as the setting for
Shakespeare's *Romeo and Juliet*, this
elegant historic town *(see pp26–7)*,
20 km (12 miles) from the lake,
features an attractive pedestrianized
centre. Spectacular Roman ruins
such as the Arena nestle among the
cobbled lanes cheek-by-jowl with
medieval palaces, a magnificent
castle in the Castelvecchio and an
array of wine bars and trattorias.

10 Monte Baldo
**MAP S3 ■ Rifugio Novezzina:
Via Generale Graziani 10, Ferrara di
Monte Baldo, 045 624 7288**

Take the cable car from Malcesine
for the 20-minute journey up the
mountain and spectacular views
from the revolving pods *(see p55)*.
At the top, there's a ski area and
a snowboarding park, as well as a
good network of hiking and biking
trails. Several mountain huts offer
refreshments and accommodation,
including Rifugio Novezzina, attached
to the Monte Baldo botanical gardens.

Garda's beach, with mountain views

A DAY TRIP FROM SALÒ TO RIVA

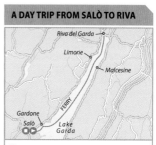

▶ MORNING

Salò is a good base for visiting
the different sections of Lake
Garda. Leave the comfortable
lakeside town on a mid-morning
fast boat service to **Riva del
Garda**. There will be a supple-
ment to the normal return
ferry price, available at the
landing stage. The boat will
pull in at the neighbouring
town of **Gardone** for views of
more Liberty villas and Grand
Hotels. The following stop
won't be for over half an hour
as you cruise up the lake to the
more rugged terrain where the
mountains drop steeply down to
the water. From your vantage
point on board, check out pretty
but crowded **Malcesine** on the
eastern shore, and then the
popular resort of **Limone** *(see
p91)* back on the west. Hop off
the boat at **Riva del Garda** *(see
p94)* and explore the town centre,
comparing the Teutonic culture
to the distinctly more Italian
atmosphere you left further down
the lake. **Restel de Fer** *(Via Restel
de Fer 10; 046 455 3481)* is a good
choice for lunch.

AFTERNOON

After lunch, wander around the
grounds of the Rocca or visit
the Museo Civico inside the building. You can also go through the
gardens to the local beaches for
a refreshing dip in the cool waters
of the lake. The return boat leaves
in the late afternoon to whisk you
back to **Salò** along the same route,
leaving you with just about enough
energy to explore the rest of the
lake the following day.

See map on p90 ◀

The Best of the Rest

1 Arco

MAP S2 ▪ Tourist Office:
Viale Delle Palme 1 ▪ 0464 532 255
▪ www.gardatrentino.it
This winter resort, the centre
of rock climbing for the area, is
topped by a 12th-century castle.

2 Bardolino
MAP R5 ▪ Tourist Office:
Piazzale Aldo Moro, Bardolino ▪ 045
721 0078 ▪ www.gardatrentino.it
Bardolino is the place to stock up
on local wine and the region's
excellent olive oil (see p56).

3 Casa di Giulietta, Verona

This homage to Shakespeare,
or to love, started in the 1930s.
Join the crowds and stick love
notes on the wall (see p27).

4 Torbole sul Garda
MAP S2 ▪ Tourist Office:
Lungolago Conca d'Oro 25 ▪ 0464
505 177 ▪ www.gardatrentino.it
A popular windsurfing destination,
Torbole has a pretty harbour
guarded by an old customs house.

5 Riva del Garda
MAP S2 ▪ Tourist Office: Largo
Medaglie d'Oro 5 ▪ 0464 554 444
▪ www.gardatrentino.it
Riva's lakefront piazza is framed by
porticoed buildings. To the east, a
castle marks the start of the town's
gardens and long stretch of beaches.

6 Lake Ledro
MAP R2 ▪ www.vallediledro.com
Surrounded by mountains, Ledro
is the highest of the Northern
Italian pre-Alpine lakes.

7 Bagolino
MAP Q2 ▪ www.bagolinoinfo.it
Tucked away in the mountains
above Lake Idro, this is a good
base for trekking in summer
and skiing in winter. During
the Lenten Carnival, masked
dancers and musicians take
to the streets.

**Bottle of
Bardolino**

8 Punta San Vigilio
This dreamy spot (see p51)
with a cypress-lined path has
an attractive pay beach.

9 Desenzano
MAP Q5 ▪ Tourist
Office: Via Porto Vecchio 34
▪ 0309 991 351 ▪ Open daily
The town of Desenzano (see p35)
has the most buzzing nightlife
around Lake Garda in the summer.

10 Torri del Benaco
MAP R4 ▪ Tourist Office:
Via Gardesana 5; 045 629 6482
▪ Museum: Viale Fratelli Lavanda
2; 045 629 6111; opening times vary,
check website; adm; www.museodel
castelloditorridelbenaco.it
The Castello Scaligero at this resort
holds a *limonaia* (glass house for
growing citrus fruits) and a museum.

Placid corner of Torri del Benaco

Garda's Parks and Gardens

Lush vegetation in Heller Garden

1 Heller Garden, Gardone
MAP Q4 ▪ Via Roma 2, Gardone Riviera, Lake Garda ▪ 336 410 877 ▪ Open Mar–Oct: 9am–7pm daily ▪ Adm ▪ www.hellergarden.com

Established in 1901, this oasis *(see p45)* is now owned by artist André Heller, who added contemporary sculptures by Roy Lichtenstein and Keith Haring.

2 Giardino di Casa Biasi
MAP R4 ▪ Via Boldiera 144, 37013 Pesina di Caprino Veronese ▪ 33 94 91 3811 ▪ Open May–Oct by reservation only ▪ www.giardinodicasabiasi.it

Owned by the Biasi family, this botanical garden is home to a variety of stunning Mediterranean flora.

3 Il Vittoriale, Gardone Riviera
MAP Q4 ▪ Via del Vittoriale 12 ▪ 0365 296 511 ▪ Open end Mar–end Oct: 9am–8pm daily (end Oct–end Mar: to 5:30pm) ▪ Adm ▪ www.vittoriale.it

The eccentric imagination of poet Gabriele d'Annunzio characterizes the grounds around his residence.

4 Isola del Garda
MAP Q4 ▪ 328 612 6943 ▪ Open May–Oct; closed Mon ▪ Adm ▪ www.isoladelgarda.com

The lake's largest island has formal gardens and a 20th-century villa.

5 Olive Groves, Sirmione
Stop for a break among the olive groves that line the route to the Grotte di Catullo *(see p35)*.

6 Public Garden, Arco
MAP S2 ▪ Viale delle Palme

This beautiful public garden harbours palms, exotic plants and Mediterranean scents.

7 Parco Baia delle Sirene, Punta San Vigilio
The Siren's Bay on Punta San Vigilio is a lovely spot *(see p51)* among olive groves, with a sheltered bay looking across to the mountains.

8 Parco Giardino Sigurtà, Valeggio sul Mincio
MAP R6 ▪ Via Cavour 1 ▪ 045 637 1033 ▪ Open Mar–Nov: 9am–7pm daily ▪ Adm ▪ www.sigurta.it

This park of mature trees and lawns is landscaped with a huge variety of flowers, such as tulips and hyacinths.

Pond in Parco Giardino Sigurtà

9 Parco Grotta Cascata Varone, North of Riva
MAP S2 ▪ Via Cascata 12, Tenno, Riva del Garda ▪ 0464 521 421 ▪ Open daily ▪ Adm ▪ www.cascata-varone.com

A series of walkways suspends you over the spectacular gorge.

10 Giardino Giusti, Verona
MAP H4 ▪ Open daily ▪ Adm

The Giardino Giusti was laid out in the 15th century as formal gardens with fountains and shady bowers.

See map on p90 ←

Sport and Relaxation

Rock climbing around Arco

1 Climbing
www.rockmasterfestival.com
■ Courses: www.mmove.net

The area around Arco features many bolted climbing routes. The town hosts the international Rock Master Festival in late August at the all-weather climbing stadium. Mmove, the first mountian climbing school based in Arco, offers various outdoor activities.

2 Mountain Biking
Xtreme Malcesine: www.xtrememalcesine.com ■ Bike Park Trentino: www.gardatrentino.it

Hire a bike from Malcesine and take the Monte Baldo cable car for trails of all levels. Alternatively, head north to race down the gravity trails at the bike park near Torbole.

3 Paragliding
www.tandemparagliding.eu

The thrill of flying over Lake Garda is made simple thanks to the Malcesine–Monte Baldo cable car, which whisks visitors up to an altitude of 1,760 m (5,774 ft). Tandem flights with professional instructors last 20–40 minutes.

4 Windsurfing
Europa Surf & Sail, Malcesine: www.sailgarda.com ■ Surf Segnana, Torbole: www.surfsegnana.it

Reliable morning winds can be found around Malcesine, while the best afternoon surfing is at Torbole.

5 Kayaking and SUP
Surfing Lino, Limone sul Garda: www.surfinglino.com ■ Europa, Malcesine: www.europasurf andsail.com

Paddle around a secluded bay or set off on a longer jaunt to explore Lake Garda, which has lots to offer.

6 Gardaland
MAP R5 ■ Castelnuovo del Garda, 37014 ■ 045 644 9777 ■ Opening times vary, check website ■ Adm ■ www.gardaland.it

Keep kids happy at Italy's top amusement park (see p54), where adrenaline-rush rides include the Black Hole roller coaster, the Tornado big wheel and watery Jungle Rapids.

7 Golf
Golf Club Arzaga: www.arzaga golf.it ■ Gardagolf: www.gardagolf.it

There are some excellent courses around Lake Garda's southern shores, including the 27 holes of Arzaga Golf Club and Gardagolf, one of Italy's best.

8 Walking
www.visitgarda.com

Whether it's a gentle stroll around the magnolia-lined bay at Salò or a hike in the mountains from the Monte Baldo cable car, the views make any walk memorable (see pp46–7).

9 Boat Tour
Sirmione Boats: www.sirmioneboats.it

Join a tour of the Sirmione peninsula to see the Grotte di Catullo and the castle from the water. This trip is better at sunset, when Prosecco is included.

10 Spas
Aquaria: Via Punta Staffalo 3, Sirmione; 030 916 261; open daily; adm; www.termedisirmione.com

Sirmione's thermal waters are well known for their beneficial qualities, and the town's spa facilities are a big draw. The Aquaria complex includes a year-round outdoor pool.

Places to Eat

1 Osteria Santo Cielo

MAP S3 ■ Piazza Turazza 11, Malcesine ■ 348 745 1345 ■ €

This quaint wine bar is a great place for a light meal of local cheeses or bruschetta. Excellent wine list, too.

2 La Casa degli Spiriti

MAP R4 ■ Via Monte Baldo 28, Costermano ■ 045 620 0766 ■ Closed Oct–Mar: Tue & Wed ■ €€€

With panoramic views of the lake, this restaurant serves Michelin-starred gourmet dishes.

3 Trattoria La Fiasca

MAP R5 ■ Via Santa Maria Maggiore 11, Sirmione ■ 030 990 6111 ■ Closed Wed ■ €€

Savour onion soup served in a hollowed-out loaf of bread, plus lake fish and handmade pasta.

Tortelli pasta, typical of Valeggio

4 Antica Locanda Mincio

MAP G5 ■ Borghetto, Via Buonarroti 12, Valeggio sul Mincio ■ 045 795 0059 ■ Closed Wed & Thu ■ €€

This ancient inn serves a mix of Mantuan and Veronese cooking, including Valeggio's famous *tortelli*.

5 Trattoria da Pino Due

MAP R4 ■ Via dell'Uva 17, Garda ■ 045 725 5694 ■ Closed Mon ■ €

The shady portico is the ideal spot to enjoy grilled whitefish and perch. Try the homemade *sanvigilini* biscuits.

PRICE CATEGORIES

For a three-course meal for one, with half a bottle of wine (or equivalent meal), taxes and extra charges.

€ under €35   €€ €35–60   €€€ over €60

---

6 Osteria dell'Orologio

MAP Q4 ■ Via Butturini 26, Salò ■ 0365 290 158 ■ Closed Wed ■ €

A historic inn where guests can savour a tasty meal made from local produce without breaking the bank. Grilled lake fish and pasta with duck are highlights.

7 La Rucola 2.0

MAP R5 ■ Via Strentelle 3, Sirmione ■ 030 916 326 ■ Closed Thu ■ €€€

An elegant Michelin-starred restaurant that's perfect for a special meal of seafood or meat. The various menu options include a selection of seven different raw-fish dishes.

8 Masi Tenuta Canova

MAP R5 ■ Via Delaini 1, Località Sacro Cuor, Lazise ■ 045 758 0239 ■ €€

Wine comes first at this vineyard trattoria. The seasonal menu of local dishes includes recommended pairings with Masi label wines.

9 Al Bersagliere

MAP H4 ■ Via Dietro Pallone 1, Verona ■ 045 800 4824 ■ Closed Sun & Mon ■ €€

This Slow Food-endorsed restaurant *(see p57)* serves traditional Veronese fare, such fillets of perch from Lake Garda and *bigoli* (thick spa-ghetti) with duck.

10 Ristorante Canottieri

MAP Q4 ■ Via Canottieri 1, 25087, Saló ■ 0365 520 613 ■ Closed winter D ■ €

Set in the sailing club of the Canottieri Garda Salò, this restaurant offers great value for money. Guests can tuck into a variety of delicious dishes made with fish from the lake and the sea.

See map on p90

TOP 10 Milan and Southern Lombardy

Milan surprises with its art treasures, contrasting its current role as a fashion hub. Outside the city, the agricultural lands defined by the River Po and its canals are dotted with hamlets, farmsteads and several towns with a rich cultural heritage. The Certosa is the apex of Pavia's monuments; Cremona lives off its 17th-century fame as a centre for violin-making; and Mantua has much remaining from the 14th to 17th centuries, when it was a centre of art and architecture.

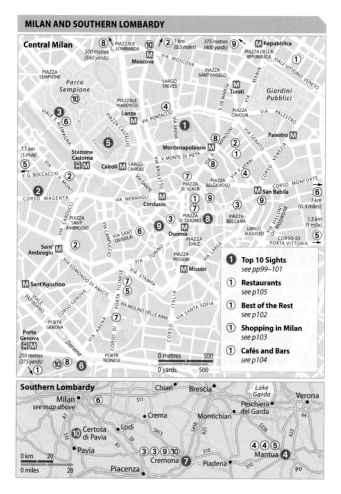

MILAN AND SOUTHERN LOMBARDY

① Top 10 Sights
see pp99–101

① Restaurants
see p105

① Best of the Rest
see p102

① Shopping in Milan
see p103

① Cafés and Bars
see p104

provides a focus for the city's contemporary design and architecture activities. Built as home to the triennial design exhibition, it now offers a selection of permanent and temporary exhibitions, a reference library, a specialist bookshop, the Caffè *(see p104)* and a buzzing bar outside in the summer.

A work by Crivelli, Pinacoteca di Brera

1 Pinacoteca di Brera, Milan

Napoleon opened this public gallery *(see pp22–3)* in 1809 to display works of art requisitioned from churches, monasteries and aristocrats throughout the north of Italy. Works include Mantegna's haunting *The Dead Christ*, Piero della Francesca's stylized *Madonna with Child, Angels, Saints and Federico da Montefeltro,* and Caravaggio's touchingly realistic *Supper at Emmaus.*

2 The Last Supper, Milan

Leonardo da Vinci finished painting *The Last Supper (see pp22–3)* on the refectory wall of the Santa Maria delle Grazie monastery in 1498. The work is outstanding for its portrayal of the disciples' emotions at the moment when Christ announces he will be betrayed. This masterpiece has survived against the odds. Using oil paint rather than watercolours meant the fresco began to disintegrate almost immediately. To add to the damage, Napoleon's troops used the wall for target practice and Allied bombs destroyed the rest of the complex, leaving just this wall standing in 1943.

3 Triennale, Milan
MAP T2 ▪ Viale Alemagna 6, Milan ▪ 02 724 341 ▪ Open 11am–6pm Tue–Sun ▪ Adm ▪ www.triennale.org
Giovanni Muzzio's exhibition space, based in the Palazzo dell'Arte (1931),

4 Palazzo Te, Mantua
MAP H6 ▪ Viale Te, Mantua ▪ 0376 323 266 ▪ Open 1–6:30pm Mon, 9am–6:30pm Tue–Sun (summer to 7:30pm) ▪ Adm ▪ www.palazzote.it
On the southern edge of the town centre, the Palazzo Te was built as a summer retreat for Federico II Gonzaga and a residence for his mistress. Begun in 1525, the Mannerist palace and gardens are a creation by Giulio Romano, inspired by the villas of ancient Rome. In the palace rooms, the stuccoed walls and ceilings create a world of their own.

5 Castello Sforzesco, Milan
The rulers of Milan, the Visconti, began construction of this castle *(see p22)* in 1368, but it was under Ludovico Sforza that it became the centre of Milan's Renaissance court, employing artists such as da Vinci and Bramante. These days the castle's museums are the main draw, with a wealth of art taken from Lombardy's churches by Napoleon's troops, furniture and Michelangelo's touching, unfinished *Pietà.*

Courtyard of the Castello Sforzesco

Milan's Navigli District at dusk

RICE

Rice was introduced to Italy during the Middle Ages from Asia. Southern Lombardy's flat plains and climate proved ideal for rice cultivation, with sunny summers and plentiful water. Rice is found on the plates of Italian homes in the form of risotto.

6 Navigli District, Milan

The mighty Naviglio Grande and the Naviglio Pavese *(see p22)* lead off from the Darsena, or basin, down to the River Po, which flows to the Adriatic Sea. The canal-side area was a working neighbourhood with *case ringhiera* (tenement housing), warehouses and factories. Since the canals fell out of use in the 1970s, the area has gradually become a focus for the city's nightlife, with bars and eateries lining the waterways. There are also a number of crafts workshops and galleries in the old courtyards.

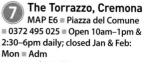

Clock in the bell tower of Cremona's Torrazzo

7 The Torrazzo, Cremona

MAP E6 ■ Piazza del Comune ■ 0372 495 025 ■ Open 10am–1pm & 2:30–6pm daily; closed Jan & Feb: Mon ■ Adm

At 112 m (413 ft) high, the Torrazzo is the tallest bell tower in Europe. Dating back to the mid-13th century, the tower is topped with a Gothic *ghirlanda* (spire). The 502 steps to the top lead to wonderful views over the Po plain.

8 Duomo, Milan

Milan's monumental cathedral *(see pp22–5)* presides over the central Piazza del Duomo, a huge square lined with stately porticoes. The piazza was created by clearing medieval streets and buildings in the 1800s to provide a better view of the church. To this day, the Duomo remains the city's social and geographical hub.

The Gothic spires of Milan's Duomo

The exterior is a confection of lofty pinnacles, statuary and filigree marble work. No visit to Milan is complete without a trip to the roof to clamber among the spires and buttresses.

⑨ Pinacoteca Ambrosiana, Milan

MAP V4 ▪ **Piazza Pio XI 2, Milan**
▪ 02 806 921 ▪ **Open 2–6pm Tue–Fri, 10am–6pm Sat & Sun** ▪ **Adm**
▪ www.ambrosiana.eu

This gallery was founded by Cardinal Federico Borromeo in 1618 under the zealous atmosphere of the Counter-Reformation and was conceived to help educate the public of their Catholic heritage. The collection includes important works of art, quirky curios and a library of manuscripts. Some of the prize exhibits were collected by the Cardinal himself, including a preparatory cartoon by Raphael, while others, such as Leonardo da Vinci's *Codex Atlanticus,* were added later.

Statuary, Pinacoteca Ambrosiana

⑩ Certosa di Pavia, Pavia

MAP C5 ▪ **Via del Monumento 4, Pavia** ▪ **Open Apr: 9–11:30am & 2:30–5:30pm Tue–Sun; May–Sep: 9–11:30am & 2:30–6pm Tue–Sun; Oct–Mar: 9–11:30am & 2:30–4:30pm Tue–Sat, 9–11am & 2:30–5pm Sun** ▪ **Tips welcomed** ▪ www.certosadipavia.com

This charterhouse complex, founded in 1396 as a mausoleum for the Visconti family, is worth visiting not just for its splendid architecture but also for the insight into the daily lives of this meditative order. A compulsory guided tour takes visitors through the tombs and artwork and out to the closed areas of the monastery.

A DAY IN CENTRAL MILAN

▶ MORNING

Start the day in **Piazza del Duomo** to visit the city's Gothic cathedral. Don't miss the surreal experience of wandering among statues and spires on the roof terraces. Back at ground level, stop for a coffee at **Zucca/Caffè Miani** *(see p104)*, on the corner of **Galleria Vittorio Emanuele II**. Walk through the elegant arcade, then wait your turn to carry out the good-luck tradition of turning three times with your heel on the genitals of the bull mosaic. Leaving the Galleria at the other end, find **La Scala** *(see p22)*, the famous opera house, just a few steps away. Take the road alongside it to reach the **Pinacoteca di Brera** *(see p99)* and spend the rest of the morning admiring the artworks. From here, it's a short walk to **Parco Sempione** *(see p23)*, behind the **Castello Sforzesco** *(see p99)*. Pick up a *panino* and have a picnic on the park's grassy lawns.

AFTERNOON

After lunch, visit the castle, taking your pick of its thematic museums (one ticket is valid for all). Back outside, take Metro line 2 from the Lanza stop to **Porta Genova**. From here, it's a short walk to the **Navigli District**, the perfect base for the rest of the day. Stroll around the atmospheric canal district, browsing the arts and craft shops and stopping for a drink along the way. Head to **El Brellin** *(see p105)* for a delicious dinner of *risotto alla Milanese* and some excellent local wines.

See map on p98

Best of the Rest

 Museo Bagatti Valsecchi, Milan

MAP X3 ▪ Via Gesù 5 ▪ Open 1–5:45pm Thu–Fri (from 10am Sat & Sun) ▪ Adm ▪ www.museobagattivalsecchi.org

This museum houses 16th-century carvings, tapestries and furniture.

Red room, Museo Bagatti Valsecchi

 Sant'Ambrogio, Milan

MAP U4

This important 12th-century church (see p22) houses the remains of the city's patron saint.

 Duomo, Cremona

MAP E6 ▪ Piazza del Comune ▪ 0372 27386 ▪ Open 8am–noon & 3:30–5:30pm Mon–Sat, 7:30am–12:30pm & 3–5pm Sun

The Romanesque Duomo in Cremona has a splendid façade with a huge rose window.

④ **Palazzo Ducale, Mantua**

MAP H6 ▪ Piazza Sordello 40 ▪ Open 8:15am–7:15pm Tue–Sun ▪ Adm ▪ www.mantovaducale.beniculturali.it

During the Renaissance, this *palazzo* was the heart of the court of Ludovico II Gonzaga.

⑤ **Basilica di San Lorenzo Maggiore, Milan**

MAP V5 ▪ Corso di Porta Ticinese 35 ▪ Open 8am–12:30pm & 3–6pm Mon–Fri; 9am–1pm & 3–7pm Sat & Sun ▪ www.sanlorenzomaggiore.com

This ancient church has an octagonal plan, well lit by the windows.

 Idroscalo, Milan

MAP C4 ▪ www.idroscalo.org

In the summer months, the city's "beach", near Linate Airport, offers swimming areas and picnic sites.

⑦ **La Scala, Milan**

Milan's internationally renowned opera house (see p22) hosts the world's top performers.

⑧ **Museo Poldi Pezzoli, Milan**

MAP W3 ▪ Via Manzoni 12 ▪ Open 10am–1pm & 2–6pm Wed–Mon ▪ Adm ▪ www.museopoldipezzoli.it

Gian Giacomo Poldi Pezzoli's collection of armoury, porcelain, jewellery, tapestries and paintings is found here.

 Museo del Violino, Cremona

MAP E6 ▪ Piazza Marconi 5 ▪ Open 11am–5pm Wed–Fri, 10am–6pm Sat & Sun ▪ Adm ▪ www.museodelviolino.org

The museum highlights five centuries of violin-making, with model instruments crafted by master violin-makers, multimedia installations and a wealth of documents.

⑩ **Parco Sempione, Milan**

MAP U2 ▪ Torre Branca: Guided tours only: Mon, Wed & Fri at 10am & 5pm; adm; www.museobranca.it ▪ Aquarium: open Tue–Sun; adm; www.acquariocivicomilano.eu

This popular park is home to the Torre Branca and an aquarium.

Monumental arch, Parco Sempione

Shopping in Milan

Crowds in Milan's elegant, light-filled Galleria Vittorio Emanuele II

1 Galleria Vittorio Emanuele II
MAP W3

This lofty 19th-century mall (see p23) offers a mixture of cafés, elegant old boutiques and expensive tourist paraphernalia.

2 Quadrilatero d'Oro
MAP X2

Exquisite boutiques from the world's top fashion houses lead off the pedestrianized lanes (see p22).

3 Corso Vittorio Emanuele II
MAP X3

If the exclusive designer boutiques of the Golden Quad are out of your budget, there are flagship stores of Italy's high-street favourites here.

4 Brera and Moscova
MAP V2

Wandering around the quirky neighbourhoods of Brera and Moscova, you will discover specialist shops, stylish boutiques and gourmet delicatessens on every corner.

5 Mercato Wagner and Street Markets
MAP C4 ▪ Mercato Wagner: Open 8am–1pm & 3:30–7:30pm Tue–Sat, mornings only Mon

Daily street markets are a feast of fresh produce; the tourist offices have addresses. Mercato Wagner offers fruit, vegetables, cheeses and cold meats under one colourful roof.

6 Outlets
MAP C4 ▪ Il Salvagente, Via Bronzetti 16 ▪ Open 3–7:30pm Mon, 10am–7:30pm Tue–Sun (closed 2–3pm Sun)

Milan is dotted with outlets and factory shops, selling everything from designer labels to discount knitwear.

7 Corso di Porta Ticinese
MAP U5

The Corso di Porta Ticinese is the heart of Milan's alternative and trend fashion scene.

8 Spazio Armani
MAP W2 ▪ Via Manzoni 31

A chic mall dedicated to different Giorgio Armani ranges, from clothing to houseware. There is also a slick café and a Japanese restaurant.

9 Furniture and Design
MAP X3 ▪ Around San Babila

For furniture and design showrooms, head to the streets leading off San Babila. Via Durini and Corso Europa are best for contemporary furniture and design classics; Corso Monforte has a host of lighting specialists.

10 Antiques Fairs
Mercatone del Naviglio Grande: MAP T6 ▪ Via Fiori Chiari: MAP V2

The last Sunday of the month sees the canalside lined with the Mercatone del Naviglio Grande. Via Fiori Chiari in Brera hosts a fair for smaller antiques on the third Sunday of the month.

See map on p98 ←

Cafés and Bars

Rita
MAP T6 ▪ Via Angelo
Fumagalli 1, Milan

Tucked away off the Naviglio Grande,
this popular spot is one of the city's
best *aperitivo* bars. Baristas shake up
excellent cocktails to be enjoyed with
delicious nibbles.

Chocolat
MAP U3 ▪ Via Boccaccio 9,
Milan

A modern coffee bar round the
corner from *The Last Supper*,
offering a selection of homemade
ice creams. In winter, the hot
chocolate is divine.

3 Portici del Comune
MAP E6 ▪ Piazza del Comune 2,
Cremona ▪ Closed Tue in winter

The outdoor tables at this bar offer
unbeatable views of the façade of
the Duomo and the central piazza
of Cremona. The coffee is among
the best served in town.

4 Cova
MAP X3 ▪ Via Montenapoleone
8, Milan ▪ 02 7600 5599

This tearoom and *pasticceria* (pastry
shop) has been run by the same
family since 1817. The chocolates
are exquisite, as is the Christmas
panettone (candied-peel bread).

5 Alla Buca della Gabbia
MAP H6 ▪ Via Cavour 98,
Mantua ▪ Open Fri–Sun

A snug little wine bar just round
the corner from Piazza Sordello
in Mantua makes the perfect
spot to settle down for a glass
of wine or an after-dinner drink.

6 Caffè Triennale
MAP T2 ▪ La Triennale, Viale
Alemagna 6, Milan ▪ Closed Mon

A slick café-restaurant, with
designer chairs, and a stylish
clientele. There's also a modish
rooftop restaurant overlooking
Parco Sempione.

7 Zucca/Caffé Miani
MAP W3 ▪ Galleria Vittorio
Emanuele II 21, Milan ▪ Closed Mon

Sip an *aperitivo* while taking in the
lovely Art Deco mosaics at one of
Milan's most famous bars. Opt for
a house Campari, invented here
in the 1860s.

**Zucca, a historic Art Deco bar in the
Galleria Vittorio Emanuele II**

8 oTTo
MAP V2 ▪ Via Paolo Sarpi 8,
Milan

A trendy aperitivo bar in Milan's
"China Town". Make sure to catch
a seat before dinner for large food
buffets accompanied by cocktails
and wine.

9 Luini
MAP W3 ▪ Via Radegonda 16,
Milan ▪ 02 8646 1917 ▪ Closed Sun
& Mon pm

Just steps away from the Duomo,
Luini serves *panzerotti* (deep-fried
mini calzone) to the queuing crowd –
try the tomato and mozzarella filling.
Standing room only.

10 Radetsky Cafè
MAP V1 ▪ Corso Garibaldi
105, Milan

This stylish bar in the hip Moscova
neighbourhood is a good pit stop
at any time. Beat regulars to the
couple of tables on the pavement
outside and watch Milan go by.

Restaurants

1 Joia
MAP Y1 ▪ Via Panfilo Castaldi 18, Milan ▪ 02 2952 2124 ▪ Closed Sun ▪ €€€

A Michelin-starred establishment serving beautifully presented vegetarian cuisine with an Asian twist.

2 Ex Mauri
MAP C4 ▪ Via Confalonieri 5 ▪ 02 6085 6028 ▪ Closed Sat L & Sun ▪ €€

With bare brick walls and eclectic furnishings, this restaurant offers traditional Italian dishes.

3 Ristorante Cracco
MAP W3 ▪ Via Victor Hugo 4, Mantua ▪ 02 876 774 ▪ Closed Sat L, Sun ▪ €€€

Michelin-starred chef Carlo Cracco produces some of the city's best Milanese dishes with a twist.

4 Il Cigno dei Martini
MAP H6 ▪ Piazza d'Arco 1, Mantua ▪ 0376 327 101 ▪ Closed Mon & Tue ▪ €€

This elegant restaurant (see p57) occupies a 16th-century palazzo with a little garden, and serves diners a range of seasonal specialities.

5 Masuelli San Marco
MAP C4 ▪ Viale Umbria 80, Milan ▪ 02 5518 4138 ▪ Closed Sun, Mon L & Aug ▪ €€

For delicious Milanese food and atmosphere, this is the best choice, located just a taxi ride from the city centre. The menu includes tripe, rice and meat dishes.

Dining room at Masuelli San Marco

6 Trattoria Milanese dal 1933
MAP V4 ▪ Via Santa Marta 11, Milan ▪ 02 8645 1991 ▪ Closed Sun ▪ €€

This elegant restaurant (see p57) serves up hearty Milanese staples. Try their creamy *risotto alla Milanese*.

7 Cantina della Vetra
MAP V5 ▪ Via Pio IV, 3 Milan ▪ 02 8940 3843 ▪ €€

Gnocchi fritti (fried potato balls) are the speciality at this bustling trattoria.

Inside Milan's Cantina della Vetra

8 El Brellin
MAP T6 ▪ Vicolo dei Lavandai, Alzaia Naviglio Grande 14, Milan ▪ 02 5810 1351 ▪ €€

Highlights here include *risotto alla Milanese* and *cotoletta alla Milanese*.

9 Il Liberty
MAP C4 ▪ Viale Monte Grappa 6 ▪ 02 2901 1439 ▪ Closed Sat L & Sun ▪ €€€

Attracting a largely business clientele, lunch here is excellent value with great dishes on the menu.

10 La Sosta
MAP E6 ▪ Via Sicardo 9, Cremona ▪ 0372 456 656 ▪ Closed Sun eve, Mon, 1 week Feb & 3 weeks Aug ▪ €€

Seasonal cooking includes the winter speciality of *bollito* (meat, salami and vegetables boiled in broth).

See map on p98

Streetsmart

Riding a bicycle on a typical cobbled
street in Verona

Getting Around

Arriving by Air

European budget airlines fly to cities across Italy year round at reasonable prices. They also offer good rates on flights within the country – ideal for covering multiple destinations in one trip. The Lakes area is served by several airports. **Milan Malpensa** is the largest, with domestic, European and intercontinental flights. Malpensa is about 40 km (25 miles) northwest of Milan but well connected to the city. Both terminals have railway stations and there are many bus services connecting with Milan's central station, including **Terravision** and the **Malpensa Shuttle**. From April to mid-October, **Alibus** runs a shuttle bus between Malpensa airport and Lake Maggiore.

Milan Linate, Milan's second airport, is much closer to the city centre. **ATM** bus 73, which runs every 10 minutes, links the airport to central Milan. The company also runs a service to the train station.

Bergamo's **Orio al Serio** airport, located midway between Lake Como and Lake Iseo, has an **ATB** bus service to the city centre, linking with the funicular for the historic upper town.

Verona is the nearest airport to Lake Garda. **ATV** runs a shuttle bus from the airport to the lake, as well as to central Verona.

Arriving by Train

Trenitalia and **Italo** both run high-speed trains between the main cities, including Verona, Brescia and Milan with links across Europe. Trenitalia's network of local trains is frequent but limited to certain parts of the Lakes area. There's a connection from Milan to Stresa, taking about an hour; fast trains from Milan to Como take just over 30 minutes. Trains to Desenzano on Lake Garda take just 20 minutes from Verona, an hour from Milan. Iseo is around 30 minutes by train from Brescia, where you must change to reach Bergamo, Verona or Milan.

Arriving by Road

Italy is reachable from other European countries via E-roads, the International European Road Network connecting major roads across national borders within Europe, or by national (N) and secondary (SS) roads from neighbouring France, Switzerland, Austria and Slovenia. The Italian network of motorways is run by **Autostrade per l'Italia**, and Northern Italy has good coverage. It's a toll-paying network: take a ticket as you enter the motorway and pay on leaving. To avoid queues, pay by credit or debit card at one of the dedicated booths. Take the A8 and A9 toll motorways instead of the A59 and A36, which have a complicated payment system.

Eurolines and **Flixbus** have long-distance coach services linking a range of cities throughout Europe and Italy, including Verona, Como, Milan and Bergamo.

Driving

The roads around the lakes get busy in summer, and parking can be a problem, particularly around Lake Garda. Lake Garda is better organized for drivers, with faster roads and more space for parking, but heavy traffic in the high season is common.

Parking spaces with blue lines require payment; look for the nearest meter. Parking charges can vary a lot, even between neighbouring villages. Yellow-lined parking spaces are reserved for residents, and white spaces are free unless stated otherwise.

Major cities and many of the smaller towns have limited traffic zones (ZTL). If you're staying at a hotel within these areas, ask them about access.

If you bring your own foreign-registered car into the country, you must carry a Green Card, the vehicle's registration documents, proof of car insurance, V5C registration certificate and a valid driver's licence. All non-EU-registered cars must also display a nationality sticker at the rear.

Boats and Ferries

The most enjoyable, and often fastest and most efficient, way to get around the lakes is by boat. There are regular ferry services including car ferries and hydrofoils. **Gestione Navigazione Laghi** runs ferries on lakes Maggiore, Como and Garda, including car and passenger-only ferries, with fast services for longer journeys as well as stopping services. **Navigazione Lago Iseo** operates on Lake Iseo. Both these offer a programme of special events, itineraries and cruises.

As well as single and return tickets, daily tickets for specific areas of each lake are available, such as Centro Lago or the Como branch of Lake Como, the lower or upper parts of Lake Garda, and the Italian or Swiss areas of Lake Maggiore. These can be used for multiple journeys in a day, so you can hop on and off the ferries many times within the specified area. Services are more frequent and reliable in summer, but it is best to book in advance.

Hiring a motorboat can be an exhilarating way to explore the lakes. Motorboats are widely available for hire both with or without a licence, including at **Rent Boat**, on Lake Maggiore; **Non Solo Barche**, near Como; **Nautica Bertelli**, on Lake Iseo; and **Sirmione Boats**, on Lake Garda.

Cycling

Each lake has at least some sections of dedicated cycle path. There are lots of places to hire bicycles, including **Garda Bike Shop** at Riva del Garda, **Iseo Bike** in Iseo, **P&L Wear and Rental** in Domaso, on Lake Como and **Stresa Bike Rental** in Stresa, Lake Maggiore. You can rent bicycles hourly or by the day. The northern part of Lake Como is best for cycling. Many hotels also offer free use of bicycles to their guests.

Walking

Many towns and cities are made up of narrow lanes and alleys, which are impenetrable to buses, and are often cobbled and can be steep. Although they add to the character of the place, they can be challenging for those with mobility problems.

The cities also have relatively compact historic centres that can be explored on foot, although in Milan the distances to be covered can be time-consuming; the city's metro is a good alternative for longer journeys.

There are numerous well signposted footpaths near the lakes and through the mountains, often following ancient routes and linking the lakeside villages and towns (see pp46–7).

DIRECTORY

ARRIVING BY AIR

Alibus
W safduemila.com

ATB (Bergamo)
W atb.bergamo.it

ATM (Milan)
W atm.it

ATV (Verona)
W atv.verona.it

Malpensa Shuttle
W malpensashuttle.it

Milan Linate
W milanolinate-airport.com

Milan Malpensa
W milanomalpensa-airport.com

Orio al Serio
W orioaeroporto.it

Terravision
W terravision.eu

Verona Airport
W aeroportoverona.it

ARRIVING BY TRAIN

Italo
W italotreno.it

Trenitalia
W trenitalia.com

ARRIVING BY ROAD

Autostrade per l'Italia
(840 042 121
W autostrade.it

Eurolines
W eurolines.com

Flixbus
W flixbus.com

BOATS AND FERRIES

Gestione Navigazione Laghi
W navigazionelaghi.it

Nautica Bertelli
Paratico
W nauticabertellirent.it

Navigazione Lago Iseo
W navigazionelagoiseo.it

Non Solo Barche
Cernobbio
W taxiboatcernobbio.it

Rent Boat
Verbania
W rentboatlago maggiore.it

Sirmione Boats
Sirmione
W sirmioneboats.it

CYCLING

Garda Bike Shop
Riva del Garda
W gardabikeshop.com

Iseo Bike
Iseo
W iseobike.com

P&L Wear and Rental
Domaso
(034 8310 4711

Stresa Bike Rental
Stresa
W stresabikerental.com

Practical Information

Passports and Visas

For entry requirements, including visas, consult the nearest Italian embassy or check the **Ministero degli Esteri** and the **Polizia di Stato** websites. All visitors to Italy need a valid passport. For residents of the EU, European Economic Area (EEA), the US, the UK, Switzerland, Canada, Australia, New Zealand and Israel, visas are required only for stays in excess of 90 days or for those intending to work, but check with your embassy before travelling.

Government Advice

Now more than ever, it is important to consult both your and the Italian government's advice before travelling. The **UK Foreign and Commonwealth Office**, the **US Department of State**, the **Australian Department of Foreign Affairs and Trade** and the **Italian Ministero della Salute** offer the latest information on security, health and local regulations.

Customs Information

You can find information on the laws relating to goods and currency taken in or out of Italy on the **ENIT** website (see p113). In case you're travelling outside the EU limits vary so check restrictions before departing. If you need any regular medication, bring enough with you and keep a copy of your prescription.

Insurance

We recommend that you take out a comprehensive insurance policy covering theft, loss of belongings, medical care, cancellations and delays and read the small print carefully. EU and Australian citizens registered to **Medicare**, or carrying a valid European Health Insurance Card (**EHIC**) or UK Global Health Insurance Card (**GHIC**) are entitled to free emergency healthcare in Italy, but prescriptions and non-emergency healthcare must be paid for.

Health

Italy has a worldclass healthcare system. If you have an EHIC or GHIC, be sure to present this in a medical emergency. You may have to pay after treatment and reclaim the money later. For visitors from outside the EU and Australia, payment of expenses is the patient's responsibility.

For medical care, go to the casualty department (pronto soccorso) at a hospital, but be prepared to wait unless it's an emergency.

No vaccinations are necessary for visiting Italy, and there are no particular health hazards in the Lakes region. Check the **Ministry of Health** website for any updates. A pharmacy (farmacie) is the best place to go for minor problems, as they give well-informed advice and sell over-the-counter medication. When closed, the name and address of the nearest out-of-hours pharmacy will be displayed outside.

It is safe to drink tap water and water from fountains unless you see a sign that it is not drinkable (non potabile). For information regarding COVID-19 vaccination requirements, consult government advice. No other vaccinations are required to enter Italy, but routine vaccines should be kept up-to-date.

Smoking, Alcohol and Drugs

Smoking is banned in enclosed public places and the possession of illegal drugs is prohibited and could result in a prison sentence. Italy has a strict limit of 0.05 per cent BAC (blood alcohol content) for drivers. This means that you cannot drink more than a small beer or a small glass of wine if you plan to drive. For drivers with less than three years' driving experience, and those under 21, the limit is 0.

ID

By law you must carry identification at all times in Italy. A photocopy of your passport photo page (and visa if applicable) should suffice. If you are stopped by the police you may be asked to present the original document within 12 hours.

Personal Security

Italy is a relatively safe country, and the Lakes region doesn't present any particular threats, though the usual sensible precautions should be taken with money, credit cards and valuables, especially in crowded areas.

Thefts can be reported to either the **Carabinieri** (military police) or Polizia di Stato (state police). They have offices in Lake Como, Lake Maggiore, Lake Garda and Lake Iseo. Both can issue the crime or loss reports (denuncia di furto o smarrimento) that you will need when making an insurance claim. Ask at the bus, train or ferry station for items left on public transport. Depending on the type of emergency, it is best to call the relevant **emergency** service.

As a rule, Italians are very accepting of all people, regardless of their race, gender or sexuality. Homosexuality was legalized in 1887 and in 1982, Italy became the third country to recognize the right to legally change your gender. If you feel unsafe, the **Safe Space Alliance** pinpoints your nearest place of refuge.

Women may receive unwanted and unwelcome attention, especially around tourist areas. If you feel threatened, head straight for the nearest police station.

Travellers with Specific Requirements

Italian airports and railway stations have well-organized assistance for travellers with impaired mobility. While large hotels have wheelchair facilities, bars and restaurants are often lacking. Smaller hillside villages can be hard to navigate due to steep, narrow lanes and flights of steps. The **AIAS**, **MilanoPerTutti** in Milan and the **Italian Tourist Board** provide information and general assistance for travellers with specific requirements.

Time Zone

Italy operates on Central European Time (CET), which is 1 hour ahead of Greenwich Mean Time and 6 hours ahead of US Eastern Standard Time. The clock moves forward 1 hour during daylight saving time from the last Sunday in March until the last Sunday in October.

Money

Italy's currency is the euro. Most establishments accept major credit, debit and pre-paid currency cards. Contactless payments are increasingly common in Italy, but it's a good idea to carry some cash for smaller items such as coffee, gelato and pizza-by-the-slice, and when visiting markets or more remote areas. Cash is also needed for ticket machines at stations. The easiest way to get cash is to use a debit or credit card at an ATM (bancomat); these are usually found in all but the smallest villages. Commission for exchanging cash is lower at post offices than at banks, and bureaux de change usually have the least favourable rates.

Wait staff should be tipped €1–2 and hotel porters and housekeeping will expect €1 per bag or day as tip.

DIRECTORY

PASSPORTS AND VISAS

Ministero degli Esteri
w vistoperitalia.esteri.it

Polizia di Stato
w poliziadistato.it

GOVERNMENT ADVICE

Australian Department of Foreign Affairs and Trade
w smarttraveller.gov.au

Italian Ministero della Salute
w salute.gov.it

UK Foreign and Commonwealth Office
w gov.uk/foreign-travel-advice

US Department of State
w travel.state.gov

INSURANCE

EHIC
w ec.europa.eu

GHIC
w ghic.org.uk

Medicare
w humanservices.gov.au

HEALTH

Ministry of Health
w salute.gov.it

PERSONAL SECURITY

Ambulance
📞 118

Carabinieri
📞 112
w carabinieri.it

Fire Services
📞 115

General Emergency
📞 112

Safe Space Alliance
w safespacealliance.com

TRAVELLERS WITH SPECIFIC REQUIREMENTS

AIAS
w aiasnazionale.it

Italian Tourist Board
w italia.it

MilanoPerTutti
w milanopertutti.it

Electrical Appliances

Italy's power supply is 230 volts. Italian plugs have two round pins; remember to bring an adaptor if required.

Mobile Phones and Wi-Fi

Visitors travelling to Italy with EU tariffs are able to use their devices abroad without being affected by roaming charges. Those from other nations will find it cheaper to invest in a pay-as-you-go Italian SIM card. **TIM**, **Vodafone**, and **Wind Tre** are the main providers. Top-ups can be bought from tobacconists *(tabacchi)* and newsstands.

Area dialling codes (starting with 0) must be used even for local calls; Italian mobile phone numbers begin with 3. International country codes should be preceded by 00 (UK 44, Australia 61), followed by the local area code minus the initial zero and the number. For the USA and Canada, dial 001, followed by the full number.

Wi-Fi is common at hotels in the area. It is also frequently available at cafés and bars, and usually also offered on high-speed trains and at the Autogrill motorway service stations. The **WiFi Italia** app allows you to connect to free hotspots throughout Italy.

Postal Services

The flat rate for sending letters and cards is €1 within Europe and €2.20 to North America. Stamps *(francobolli)* can be bought at *tabacchi*, recognizable by a large blue or black "T" sign or at post offices. You can find a complete list of post offices on the **Poste Italiane** website. Post boxes are red and can be found in all towns and villages. Avoid using the pre-franked postcards that are sometimes sold in touristy places – they generally cost more and take longer to be delivered.

Weather

The areas around the Italian Lakes have a generally mild climate despite their proximity to the mountains. Winters can be rainy and cold, however, and most of the villas and gardens, as well as many hotels and restaurants, close between November and February. The best months to visit are May and June, and again in September, when the weather is still summery.

Opening Hours

Shops and banks usually open around 8 or 9am. They close at 12:30 or 1pm until 3:30 or 4pm, then they remain open until about 7:30pm (banks close earlier). Non-stop opening hours *(orario continuato)* are becoming more widespread, however. Banks are usually closed on Saturday afternoons and on Sunday, while many shops are open daily, especially in popular resorts. Most museums open Tuesday to Sunday, and last entry is usually 30 minutes before the official closing time.

COVID-19 Increased rates of infection may result in temporary opening hours and/or closures. Always check ahead before visiting museums, attractions and hospitality venues.

Visitor Information

ENIT is the national tourist board, and the website has useful information and links. There are tourist offices in the main towns and villages around the lakes, including **Lake Iseo and Franciacorta**, **Lake Como**, **Lake Maggiore** and **Lake Garda**, which provide information on accommodation and attractions, sell discount cards and sometimes deal with bookings.

Many companies offer themed tours of the Lakes area. **ProntoGuide** has many itineraries, such as culinary tours, guided local experiences through the Borromean Islands and Lago Maggiore, and day trips to Orta San Giulio and the Sacro Monte.

Local Customs

Italians are rather relaxed when it comes to etiquette. Strangers shake hands, while friends and family greet each other with a kiss on both cheeks. But there are some strict rules. Visitors may be fined for littering, drinking and eating outside churches and monuments. It's an offence to bathe in public fountains. There are also fines for buying items from illegal traders on the street.

Strict dress codes apply inside churches: cover your torso and upper arms, and ensure shorts and skirts cover your knees. Shoes must be worn. In some places of worship photography is not allowed.

Language

The official language is Italian, but there are many regional languages spoken, such as Friulian, Sardinian, Piedmontese and Sicilian.

The level of English and other foreign languages spoken can be limited, particularly in rural areas, and locals appreciate efforts to speak Italian, even if only a few words.

Taxes and Refunds

VAT (called IVA in Italy) is usually 22 per cent, with a reduced rate of 4 to 10 per cent on some items. Non-EU citizens can claim an IVA refunds on goods costing a combined total of at least €155 (bought from the same store on the same day). It is easier to claim before you buy (you will need to show your passport to the shop assistant and complete a form). If claiming retrospectively, at the airport, present a customs officer with your purchases and a *fattura* (invoice), with your name and the amount of IVA on the item purchased.

Accommodation

There's a good choice of hotels of all levels in the Lakes area, plus a range of quality hotels in historic lakeside villas. Sites such as **Booking.com** have a good range of options in the area. B&Bs often

provide the best deals in terms of comfort, style, price and location, and hosts are usually keen to help with local advice. **BBcard** is a website with a good range of the B&Bs provide a discount card for stays at member establishments; **Ospiti per Casa** has a number of attractive B&Bs on Lake Como. **Homestay** provides a selection of hosts offering private rooms, usually simple and inexpensive.

Agriturismi are working farms with a restaurant, pleasant accommodation or both, and sometimes they also offer activities and farm experiences. Campsites are a popular option for lakeside holidays, since they often have direct access to the water, and there is a fair selection of self-catering apartments and villas.

In addition to well-known online booking organizations such as **Airbnb**, there are some very good rental agencies, like **Apartments Garda Lake** (Lake Garda) and **Cozy Homes Lago Maggiore**.

Direct booking is favoured by many of the smaller hotels. Breakfast, parking and facilities such as wellness areas and bicycles may or may not be included in the price; it's a good idea to check before booking. One extra cost that is not down to the individual hotel is the *tassa di soggiorno*, a municipal tax imposed on the first four nights you stay at an establishment in some areas in Italy. Depending on the local regulations and the type of establishment, this tax varies from around 60 cents to €5 per night per person.

DIRECTORY

MOBILE PHONES AND WI-FI

TIM
W tim.it

Vodafone
W vodafone.it

WiFi Italia
W wifi.italia.it

Wind Tre
W windtre.it

POSTAL SERVICES

Poste Italiane
W poste.it

VISITOR INFORMATION

ENIT
W italia.it

Lake Como
W lakecomo.it

Lake Garda
W visitgarda.com

Lake Iseo & Franciacorta
W iseolake.info

Lake Maggiore
W illagomaggiore.com

ProntoGuide
W guidelaghi.it

ACCOMMODATION

Airbnb
W airbnb.com

Apartments Garda Lake
W apartmentsgarda lake.it

BBcard
W bbcard.it

Booking.com
W booking.com

Cozy Homes Lago Maggiore
W cozyhomes-lago maggiore.it

Homestay
W homestay.com

Ospiti per Casa
W ospitipercasa.com

Places to Stay

Luxury Hotels

Casa Museo Palazzo Valenti Gonzaga

MAP H6 ▪ Via Pietro Frattini 7, 46100 Mantova ▪ 348 441 9954 ▪ www. valentigonzaga.com ▪ €€

This 17th-century hotel is part of the Italian Historic House Association and features its own museum of 1600s art. The stone walls, original frescoes and antique furniture make any stay a truly unique experience.

L'Albereta

MAP E4 ▪ Via Vittorio Emanuele 23, Erbusco, Franciacorta ▪ 030 776 0550 ▪ www.albereta.it ▪ €€€

There's a peaceful atmosphere at this country house hotel owned by the Bellavista winery. Rooms feature fireplaces, frescoes and balconies, plus antique furniture and quality fabrics. The hotel spa and restaurants are added luxuries.

Grand Hotel Fasano e Villa Principe

MAP Q4 ▪ Corso Zanardelli 190, Gardone Riviera, Lake Garda ▪ 0365 290 220 ▪ Closed Oct–Easter ▪ www.ghf.it ▪ €€€

The extensive park at this opulent villa hotel dating from Gardone's heyday has palms and a pool with lake views. The spacious public rooms are formal, and the bedrooms are classically decorated.

Grand Hotel Tremezzo

MAP N3 ▪ Via Regina 8, Tremezzo, Lake Como ▪ 0344 42491 ▪ www. grandhoteltremezzo.com ▪ €€€

Ideally located to explore Villa Carlotta, this stylish Art Nouveau hotel has exceptional facilities such as a floating swimming pool and the lake's best spa. Rooms are decorated with period furniture, brocade fabrics, as well as antique prints and paintings. Lovely garden and lake views.

Grand Hotel Villa Serbelloni

MAP N3 ▪ Via Roma 1, Bellagio, Lake Como ▪ 031 950 216 ▪ www. villaserbelloni.com ▪ €€€

In an unbeatable location on Lake Como, this mid-19th-century hotel now has a Michelin-starred restaurant and two pools.

Gran Duca di York

MAP V4 ▪ Via Moneta 1, 20123 Milan ▪ 02 874 863 ▪ www.ducadiyork. com ▪ €€€

Set inside a gorgeous 19th-century building, this hotel is located near Milan's fashion district and the Duomo. Period frescoes decorate the ceilings, and the bedrooms have elegant furnishings.

Lefay Resort & Spa

MAP R3 ▪ Via Angelo Feltrinelli 136, Gargnano, Lake Garda ▪ 0365 241800 ▪ lagodigarda. lefayresorts.com ▪ €€€

A huge eco-resort, Lefay offers an award-winning spa. The excellent facilities here include indoor and outdoor heated saltwater pools, an infinity pool, five saunas, a hammam, as well as a salt lake.

Locanda San Vigilio

MAP R4 ▪ Punta San Vigilio, Garda, Lake Garda ▪ 045 725 6688 ▪ www.locanda-san vigilio.it ▪ €€€

Punta San Vigilio is one of the most bewitching corners in the Lakes region. The exclusive location has been enjoyed by the likes of Winston Churchill and King Juan Carlos of Spain in the past. Service is friendly at the Locanda, and the position – between the lake and olive groves – truly breathtaking.

Villa d'Este

MAP M4 ▪ Via Regina 40, Cernobbio, Lake Como ▪ 031 3481 ▪ Closed mid-Nov–Feb ▪ www.villadeste.it ▪ €€€

Built back in 1568 and transformed into a hotel in 1873, Villa d'Este has been a pleasure palace for much of its history. These days, wealthy guests and Hollywood celebrities visit the property to enjoy its gardens and the lakeside luxury.

Villa Feltrinelli
MAP R3 ▪ Via Rimembranza 38–40, Gargnano, Lake Garda ▪ 0365 798 000 ▪ Closed mid-Oct–mid-Apr ▪ www.villafeltrinelli.com ▪ €€€
One of the world's best hotels, this Liberty villa has a pool and grounds leading to Lake Garda. Its 13 rooms and handful of suites are elegantly furnished with antiques.

Villa Sostaga
MAP R3 ▪ Via Sostaga 19, Gargnano, Lake Garda ▪ 0365 791 218 ▪ www.villasostaga.com ▪ €€€
Set on a hillside above Lake Garda, Villa Sostaga has stunning views. The rooms are furnished with period pieces, and there are extensive grounds with a swimming pool. The well-priced restaurant serves meals on the terrace in summer.

Villa della Torre
MAP S5 ▪ Via della Torre 25, Fumane di Valpolicella ▪ 045 683 2070 ▪ www.villadellatorre.it ▪ €€€
This Renaissance villa in the Valpolicella area is owned by the Allegrini winemaking dynasty. Choose between the refined Art rooms or the country-style Wine rooms, with beamed ceilings. Don't miss the statuesque fireplaces.

Hotels and B&Bs by the Lakes

Casa Visnenza
MAP F2 ▪ Via S. Faustino 7, Capo di Ponte ▪ 320 906 4557 ▪ www.casavisnenza.com ▪ €
Set in a former silk mill, this B&B is located near the prehistoric rock carvings of Val Camonica. Wood and stone interiors and antique furniture add to Casa Visnenza's charm. The friendly owners organize activities, including food tours.

Grifone
MAP R5 ▪ Via Bocchio 4, Sirmione, Lake Garda ▪ 030 916 014 ▪ www.sirmionehotelgrifone.it ▪ €
This friendly two-star hotel has an unbeatable location – down a quiet side alley by the castle, right on the lake. The breakfast buffet selection is impressive, and there's an idyllic terrace with a little beach just below.

Lago di Garda
MAP S2 ▪ Via Lungolago Conca d'Oro 11, Torbole, Lago di Garda ▪ 0464 505 111 ▪ www.hotellagodigarda.it ▪ €
The decor is generally contemporary and the views are timeless at this stylish hotel opposite the lake in Torbole. For the perfect day, make use of the spa facilities, then have breakfast on the summer terrace and come back after a day of sightseeing to unwind and dine at the Aqua restaurant.

Albergo Milano
MAP N2 ▪ Via XX Settembre 35, Varenna, Lake Como ▪ 0341 830 298 ▪ €€
An attractive three-star hotel tucked away in the cobbled streets of Varenna. The rooms at Albergo Milano are decorated with local antique furniture, and there's a terrace restaurant offering panoramic lake views.

Bellavista
MAP M4 ▪ Piazza Bonacossa 2, Brunate, Lake Como ▪ 031 221 031 ▪ www.bellavistabrunate.com ▪ €€
In an Art Nouveau villa just across from the funicular station, this welcoming hotel offers respite from the summer heat and crowds. It has original glass windows and sandblasted doors. There are stunning lake views from the terrace of the restaurant.

Gardesana
MAP R4 ▪ Piazza Calderini 5, Torri del Benaco, Lake Garda ▪ 045 722 5411 ▪ Closed mid-Oct–Easter ▪ www.gardesana.eu ▪ €€
This three-star hotel is set in a dreamy location at the side of the small harbour in Torri del Benaco, on Lake Garda. The decent, well-priced rooms have lovely views, and the restaurant has a lake-facing balcony. The staff in the hotel and restaurant will always make you feel welcome.

Olivi
MAP R5 ▪ Via San Pietro in Mavino 5, Sirmione, Lake Garda ▪ 030 990 5365 ▪ www.hotelolivi.com ▪ €€
The location of this hotel, a short stroll out of the town centre towards the Grotte di Catullo, is peaceful and panoramic. There's an open-air swimming pool in summer, plus indoor and outdoor naturally heated spa pools.

Posta Design Hotel

MAP M4 ▪ Via Giuseppe Garibaldi 2, Como, Lake Como ▪ 031 276 9011 ▪ www.postadesignhotel. com ▪ €€

A short walk from the train station, this stylish boutique hotel is located in the heart of Como. The contemporary rooms are decorated in shades of white and grey, and have oak wood floors and framed silk foulards adorning the walls. The cafe on site is a popular spot for an *aperitivo*.

Villa Arcadio

MAP Q4 ▪ Via Navelli, Salò ▪ 0365 42281 ▪ www. hotelvillaarcadio.it ▪ €€€

Amid fruit orchards and olive groves, this boutique hotel is housed in a former convent. The interiors are decorated with original fresco details, as well as the owners' private collection of antiques and works of art. The restaurant serves exceptional cuisine that uses fresh local ingredients.

Farm stays (Agriturismi)

Al Rocol

MAP F4 ▪ Via Provinciale 79, Ome, Franciacorta ▪ 030 685 2542 ▪ www. alrocol.com ▪ €

This lovely family-run Franciacorta winery offers simple, comfortable rooms and a small camper van area, as well as an excellent farmhouse restaurant and outdoor pool. Cookery courses and winery tours are available, and guests can meet the animals, which include donkeys and deer.

Borgo San Donino

MAP Q5 ▪ Agriturismo Borgo San Donino, Cascina Capuzza, Desenzano del Garda ▪ 030 991 0279 ▪ www. selvacapuzza.it ▪ €

This wine-making estate near Lake Garda offers several self-catering apartments with bright, wooden interiors and serene surroundings. Facilities include a swimming pool, restaurant and wine tastings.

Cascina Borgo Francone

MAP P1 ▪ Cascina Borgo Francone, Pian di Spagna, Gera Lario, Lake Como ▪ 0344 84160 ▪ www. cascinaborgofrancone. com ▪ €

This luxurious resort is located in the natural reserve of Pian di Spagna, making it an ideal location for bird-watching, horse riding and cycling. There is a spa with heated indoor swimming pool and acres of woodland to explore.

El Giardì

MAP F3 ▪ Via Monte Marone 9, Marone, Lake Iseo ▪ 030 982 7400 ▪ www.elgiardi.it ▪ €

There are exceptional lake views from this 18th-century stone farmhouse, as well as an outdoor pool with lake views and good walking opportunities. Pierangelo can accompany guests on hikes, and his wife Anna provides good home cooking.

Il Bagnolo

MAP Q4 ▪ Via Serniga, Località Bagnolo, Salò, Lake Garda ▪ 0365 20290 ▪ www.ilbagnolo.it ▪ €€

Twelve attractive rooms are available in this stylish

agriturismo on a quiet hillside above Lake Garda. The exclusive restaurant serves locally sourced food and wine.

Bersi Serlini Winery

MAP F4 ▪ Via Cereto 7, Provaglio d'Iseo, Franciacorta ▪ 030 982 3338 ▪ www.bersiserlini. it ▪ €€

There's a good mix of contemporary and historic design elements at this beautiful winery adjacent to the Torbiere nature trails. The four suites are located in a former monastery building, and guests can enjoy a free tour and tasting.

Pratello

MAP Q5 ▪ Via Pratello 26, Padenghe sul Garda, Lake Garda ▪ 030 990 7005 ▪ www.pratello. com ▪ €€

Surrounded by vines and with spectacular views over Lake Garda, the extensive grounds at this relaxing *agriturismo* in the Moreniche hills include a swimming pool, cellar and very good seasonal restaurant. Rooms and apartments sleep two to six people.

Serego Alighieri

MAP S5 ▪ Via Stazione Vecchia 472, Sant'Ambrogio di Valpolicella ▪ 045 770 3622 ▪ www. seregoalighieri.it ▪ €€

These elegantly furnished apartments are part of the historic wine estate bought by Dante Alighieri's son and still run by the poet's descendants. They feature beamed ceilings and wooden floors. Although breakfast is served, each apartment has its own kitchen.

Dimora Bolsone

MAP Q4 ▪ Via Panoramica 23, Gardone Riviera, Lake Garda ▪ 0365 21022 ▪ No under 12s ▪ www. dimorabolsone.it ▪ €€€
This renovated 15th-century manor house set among the lush hillsides of Lake Garda has bright, spacious rooms with stunning lakeside views. Extensive gardens with waterfalls and a spa water pool guarantee a wonderfully restful break. Bicycles are available for hire.

Campsites

Campeggio Villaggio Gefara

MAP N1 ▪ Via Case Sparse 230, Domaso, Lake Como ▪ 0344 96163 ▪ www.campinggefara.it ▪ €
Located at the northern end of Lake Como, this bustling campsite offers apartments, bungalows and a family cottage. The long stretch of lake beach is backed by a grassy area shaded by trees.

Camping Bellagio

MAP N3 ▪ Via Valassina 170C, Bellagio, Lake Como ▪ 031 951 325 ▪ www.bellagio-camping. com ▪ €
This is a refreshingly underdeveloped site outside Bellagio, on the hills overlooking Lake Como. Camping is in two green fields, facilities are simple, and the site is within walking distance of a village with shopping and dining options. No dogs allowed.

Camping Conca d'Oro

MAP J3 ▪ Via Quarantadue Martiri 26, Feriolo, Baveno, Lake Maggiore ▪ 0323 28116 ▪ www.concadoro.it ▪ €
A pleasant campsite on the shores of Lake Maggiore, with 250 tent pitches and caravans for hire. The beach is particularly suitable for children, since there are organized activities for under 14s. There is also a small supermarket, bar and restaurant on site.

Camping Delta

MAP L1 ▪ Via Respini 7, Locarno, Switzerland ▪ (+41) 91 751 6081 ▪ www.campingdelta. com ▪ €
This quality site on the banks of Lake Lugano has attractive grounds and good facilities. There are fitness and sports facilities, a children's playground and beach, as well as a pizzeria and garden restaurant. Kayaks and bikes are also available to rent.

Camping Isolino

MAP J3 ▪ Via Per Feriolo 25, Verbania, Lake Maggiore ▪ 0323 496 080 ▪ www.isolino.it ▪ €
A well-organized complex on the shores of Lake Maggiore, Isolino offers bungalows, tents and caravan pitches. Amenities include sports and organized activities, a water park, a private lake beach and refreshment options.

Camping Nanzel

MAP S2 ▪ Via 4 Novembre 3, Limone sul Garda ▪ 0365 954 155 ▪ www. campingnanzel.it ▪ €
A simple camping site just outside Limone,

on the northwestern shore of Lake Garda. Pitches are among olive groves, and the site has its own beach.

Camping Orta

MAP J4 ▪ Via Domodossola 28, Orta San Giulio ▪ 0322 90267 ▪ www.camping orta.it ▪ €
Less than 2 km (1 mile) outside Orta, this little site offers bungalows and caravans, as well as tent pitches. The terraced grassy pitches lead down to the road and lakeside beach.

Camping Valle Romantica

MAP K2 ▪ Via Valle Cannobina, Cannobio, Lake Maggiore ▪ 0323 71249 ▪ www.riviera-valleromantica.com ▪ €
On the riverbank, just outside Cannobio, this campsite has beautiful, mature grounds. Accommodation options include rustic apartments and modern caravans, while the café in the old farmhouse has tables outside under the wisteria.

Camping Bella Italia

MAP R5 ▪ Via Bell'Italia 2, Peschiera del Garda ▪ 045 640 0688 ▪ www. camping-bellaitalia.it ▪ €€
Within walking distance of Peschiera, on Lake Garda, this spacious site has bungalows, apartments and mobile homes, plus plenty of greenery. There is also a water park, a lakeside beach and sports and entertainment facilities.

General Index

Acknowledgments

Author

Lucy Ratcliffe is a travel writer and translator specializing in the northern Italian Lakes. For over ten years she has travelled and lived in the region, writing numerous guidebooks as well as translating texts on contemporary architecture.

Additional contributor
Sarah Lane

Publishing Director Georgina Dee

Publisher Vivien Antwi

Design Director Phil Ormerod

Editorial Ankita Awasthi Tröger, Rebecca Flynn, Rachel Fox, Maresa Manara, Alison McGill, Sands Publishing Solutions, Sally Schafer

Cover Design Richard Czapnik

Design Bhavika Mathur, Marisa Renzullo

Picture Research Taiyaba Khatoon, Sumita Khatwani, Ellen Root

Cartography Suresh Kumar, Casper Morris, Animesh Pathak, Zafar-ul-Islam Khan

Base mapping supplied by Kartographie Huber, www.kartographie.de

Senior Production Editor Jason Little

Production Igrain Roberts

Factchecker Kiki Deere

Proofreader Kathryn Glendenning

Indexer Helen Peters

Revisions team Karris Ainsworth, Ashif, Avanika, Dipika Dasgupta, Mohammed Hassan, Taiyaba Khatoon, Shikha Kulkarni, Halima Mohammed, Daniel Mosseri, Chhavi Nagpal, Anjasi Nyshadham, Bandana Paul, Vagisha Pushp, Anuroop Sanwalia, Mark Silas, Beverly Smart, Priyanka Thakur, Vinita Venugopal, Tanveer Zaidi

Commissioned Photography Helena Smith

Picture Credits

The publisher would like to thank the following for their kind permission to reproduce their photographs:
Key: a-above; b-below/bottom; c-centre; f-far; l-left; r-right; t-top

123RF.com: claudiodivizia 99br; make 86bl; mikolaj64 62b; Claudio Vidrich 44t.

4Corners: Günter Gräfenhain 12bl, 15cr, 33bl, 55t, 64clb, 69br, 77b; SIME /Gabriele Croppi 23bl, 24bc.

Alamy Stock Photo: AA World Travel Library 42cl; Marco Arduino 16bl; Augusto Colombo - ITALIA 61cl; Richard Boot 30-1; John Burnikell 28cb; Mirko Costantini 60bl; Ian G Dagnall 7t; Larisa Dmitrieva 85br; freeartist 11c, 49cr; Hemis.fr / Ludovic Maisant 101cl; Heritage Image Partnership Ltd 41tl; imageBROKER 51cl; David Keith Jones 40c; Look Die Bildagentur der Fotografen GmbH 13cb; luciopix 16crb; Giuseppe Masci 79tl; Gisella Motta 13tl; Lynne Nieman 59tr; Painting 40b; Realy Easy Star / Toni Spagone 18cra, 43tr; REDA &CO srl 97cl, 104cr; robertharding 10crb; SFM Italy E 63cl, 94c; Rick Strange 10bl; Paul Street 46cla; Universal Images Group North America LLC / DeAgostini 72clb; Steve Vidler 10tr; Jan Wlodarczyk 26bl, 50cl.

AWL Images: Jon Arnold 3tr, 11tl, 106-7; Walter Bibikow 7cr; Marco Bottigelli 1, 88br; ClickAlps 58b; Matteo Colombo 47tl; Francesco Iacobelli 4b, 48cl; Katja Kreder 55crb, Stefano Politi Markovina 23tl, 65tl, 65b, 71cl, Doug Pearson 74br; Travel Pix Collection 17tl, 46b; Catherina Unger 58tr.

Cantina della Vetra: 105cr.

Depositphotos Inc: moprand 31bl.

Dreamstime.com: Andreadonetti 57cl; Areinwald 63tr; Valentin Armianu 56br; Frank Bach 10clb; Rudy Bagozzi 39tr; Claudio Balducelli 93tl; Jennifer Barrow 100b; Cedric Bennett 11cra; Roberto Binetti 22clb; Bombaert 102br; Roberto Cerruti 11crb; Claudio Giovanni Colombo 78cl; Elizabeth Coughlan 72tr; Olena Danileiko 56tl; Olga Demchishina 45clb, 70b; Dennis Dolkens 2tr, 11bl, 36-7; Federico Donatini 52br; Efired 27crb; Elitravo 44bl; Bozza Ferdinando 31tl; Freesurf69 78-9; Giovanni Gagliardi 29bl; Jorg Hackemann 24cla; Irinafuks 47br; Ixuskmitl 28-9; Jojjik 86t; Vladimir Korostyshevskiy 38cb, 100c; Serhii Liakhevych 35tl; Olga Lupol 92-3; Marcorubino 26-7; Isso Marovich 54cl; Mineria6 68tl; Morseicinque 73b; Nadmikusova 39clb; Oktober64 20-1; Olgacov 4cr; Ciprian Salceanu 52tl; Marco Saracco 6b, 34bl; Marco Scisetti 29cr; Jozef Sedmak 4clb, 27tl, 88cla; Spongecake 103t; Tixtis 61tr; Noppasin Wongchum 25b; Xantana 2tl, 8-9, 62cl; Zkk600 92cl.

Franciacorta: 32clb.

Getty Images: AGF 95tl; Vittorio Zunino Celotto 22cra; De Agostini 84cla, / G. Berengo Gardin 70tl, / G. Cigolini 102cla, *Battle of Legnano May 29, 1176* (ca 1860) by Amos Cassioli photo G. Nimatallah 38t; mattia. bonavida@gmal.com / Moment Open 50t; Federica Grassi 49b; Heritage Images 85t; Marka 33cr, 35crb, 87cl; Nick Brundle Photography 10cl; Vincenzo Pinto 59cl; Mondadori Portfolio 19c; Olaf Protze 14cla; Mats Silvan 4t, 14-5; Flavio Vallenari 53cl.

iStockphoto.com: alxpin 91b; andrzej63 3tl; 66-7; Ardenvis 32-3; gillian-bell 91tl; ClaraNila 74tl; domin_domin 80b; Gio_tto 16-7, 18crb; luniversa 76tl; megatronservizi 53tr; megula 4cla; no_limit_pictures 43clb; olgysha2008 12-3; repistu 100tl; StevanZZ 18-9; Flavio Vallenari 34-5, 60t, 94b; xenotar 82-3.

Locanda dell'Isola Comacina: 81cl.

Masuelli San Marco: 105bl.

Pinacoteca di Brera: 23cr, *Camerino Triptych (Triptych of Saint Domenico)* (1482 - 1483) by Carlo Crivelli 99tl.

Restaurante Milano: 75cra.

Rex Shutterstock: Alinari 25tc.

Robert Harding Picture Library: Peter Barritt 19cr; Antonella Carri 30cl; Franz Marc Frei 69tl; Jurgen Wackenhut 51tr; Ernst Wrba 42tr.

Sigurta Giardino Valeggio: 95cr.

Shutterstock.com: Kvitka Fabian 4crb.

SuperStock: agf photo 45tr; Cubo Images 41br, 77tr; imageBROKER 15tl; Marka 4cl, 89cr; Prisma 96tl.

Villa Crespi: 75cb.

Cover
Front and spine: **AWL Images:** Marco Bottigelli.

Back: **Alamy Stock Photo:** Pavel Dudek crb, Joana Kruse cla, David Lyons tr; **AWL Images:** Marco Bottigelli b; **Dreamstime.com:** Boggy tl.

Pull Out Map Cover
AWL Images: Marco Bottigelli.

All other images © Dorling Kindersley

For further information see:
www.dkimages.com

Penguin Random House

First edition 2011

Published in Great Britain by
Dorling Kindersley Limited
DK, One Embassy Gardens, 8 Viaduct
Gardens, London, SW11 7BW, UK

The authorised representative in the EEA
is Dorling Kindersley Verlag GmbH.
Arnulfstr. 124, 80636 Munich, Germany

Published in the United States by
DK Publishing, 1745 Broadway, 20th Floor,
New York NY 10019, USA

A CIP catalogue record is available
from the British Library.

A catalogue record for this book is available
from the Library of Congress.

ISSN 1479-344X

ISBN 978 0 2414 6289 8

Printed and bound in China

www.dk.com

As a guide to abbreviations in visitor information blocks: **Adm** = *admission charge;* **D** = *dinner;* **L** = *lunch.*

Phrase Book

In an Emergency

Help!	Aiuto!	eye-yoo-toh
Stop!	Ferma!	fair-mah
Call a doctor.	Chiama un medico.	kee-ah-mah oon meh-dee-koh
Call an ambulance.	Chiama un' ambulanza.	kee-ah-mah oon am-boo-lan-tsa
Call the police.	Chiama la polizia.	kee-ah-mah la pol-ee-tsee-ah
Call the fire brigade.	Chiama i pompieri.	kee-ah-mah ee pom-pee-air-ee

Communication Essentials

Yes/No	Sì/No	see/noh
Please	Per favore	pair fah-vor-eh
Thank you	Grazie	grah-tsee-eh
Excuse me	Mi scusi	mee skoo-zee
Hello	Buon giorno	bwon jor-noh
Goodbye	Arrivederci	ah-ree-veh-dair-chee
Good evening	Buona sera	bwon-ah sair-ah
What?	Quale?	kwah-leh?
When?	Quando?	kwan-doh?
Why?	Perché?	pair-keh?
Where?	Dove?	doh-veh?

Useful Phrases

How are you?	Come sta?	koh-meh stah?
Very well, thank you.	Molto bene, grazie.	moll-toh beh-neh grah-tsee-eh
Pleased to meet you.	Piacere di conoscerla.	pee-ah-chair-eh dee-koh-noh-shair-lah
That's fine.	Va bene.	va beh-neh
Where is/ are …?	Dov'è/ Dove sono …?	dov-eh/doveh soh-noh…?
How do get to …?	Come faccio per Arrivare a …?	koh-meh fah-choh pair arri-var-eh ah…?
Do you speak English?	Parla inglese?	par-lah een-gleh-zeh?
I don't understand.	Non capisco.	non ka-pee-skoh
I'm sorry.	Mi dispiace.	mee dee-spee-ah-cheh

Shopping

How much does this cost?	Quant'è, per favore?	kwan-the pair fah-vor-eh?
I would like …	Vorrei …	vor-ray
Do you have …?	Avete …?	ah-veh-teh…?
Do you take credit cards?	Accettate carte di credito?	ah-chet-tah-the kar-teh dee creh-dee-toh?
What time do you open/ close?	A che ora apre/ chiude?	ah keh or-ah ah-preh/ kee-oo-deh?
this one	questo	kweh-stoh
that one	quello	kwell-oh
expensive	caro	kar-oh
cheap	a buon prezzo	ah bwon pret-soh
size, clothes	la taglia	lah tah-lee-ah
size, shoes	il numero	eel noo-mair-oh
white	bianco	bee-ang-koh
black	nero	neh-roh
red	rosso	ross-oh
yellow	giallo	jal-loh
green	verde	vair-deh
blue	blu	bloo

Types of Shop

bakery	il forno /il panificio	eel forn-oh /il /eel pan-ee-fee-choh
bank	la banca	lah bang-kah
bookshop	la libreria	lah lee-breh-ree-ah
cake shop	la pasticceria	lah pas-tee-chair-ee-ah
chemist	la farmacia	lah far-mah-chee-ah
delicatessen	la salumeria	lah sah-loo-meh-ree-ah
department store	il grande magazzino	eel gran-deh mag-gad-zee-noh
grocery	alimentari	ah-lee-men-tah-ree
hairdresser	il parrucchiere	eel par-oo-kee-air-eh
ice cream parlour	la gelateria	lah jel-lah-tair-ree-ah
market	il mercato	eel mair-kah-toh
newsstand	l'edicola	leh-dee-koh-lah
post office	l'ufficio postale	loo-fee-choh pos-tah-leh
supermarket	il supermercato	eel su-pair-mair-kah-toh
tobacconist	il tabaccaio	eel tah-bak-eye-oh
travel agency	l'agenzia di viaggi	lah-jen-tsee-ah dee vee-ad-jee

Sightseeing

art gallery	la pinacoteca	lah peena-koh-teh-kah
bus stop	la fermata dell'autobus	lah fair-mah-tah dell ow-toh-booss
church	la chiesa/ la basilica	lah kee-eh-zah/ lah bah-seel-i-kah
closed for holidays	chiuso per le ferie	kee-oo-zoh pair leh fair-ee-eh
garden	il giardino	eel jar-dee-no
museum	il museo	eel moo-zeh-oh
railway station	la stazione	lah stah-tsee-oh-neh
tourist information	l'ufficio di turismo	loo-fee-choh dee too-ree-smoh

Staying in a Hotel

Do you have any vacant rooms?	Avete camere libere?	ah-veh-teh kah-mair-eh lee-bair-eh?
double room	una camera doppia	oona kah-mair-ah doh-pee-ah
with double bed	con letto matrimoniale	kon let-toh-mah tree-moh-nee-ah-leh
twin room	una camera con due letti	oona kah-mair-ah kon doo-eh let-tee
single room	una camera singola	oona kah-mair-ah sing-goh-lah
room with a bath, shower	una camera con bagno, con doccia	oona kah-mair-ah kon ban-yoh, kon dot-chah
I have a reservation.	Ho fatto una prenotazione.	oh fat-toh oona preh-noh-tah-tsee-oh-neh

Eating Out

Have you got a table for ...?	**Avete un tavolo per ...?**	*ah-veh-teh oon tah-voh-lah pair ...?*
I'd like to reserve a table	**Vorrei riservare un tavolo.**	*vor-ray ree-sair-vah-reh oon tah-voh-lah*
breakfast	**colazione**	*koh-lah-tsee-oh-neh*
lunch	**pranzo**	*pran-tsoh*
dinner	**cena**	*cheh-nah*
The bill, please.	**Il conto, per favore.**	*eel kon-toh pair fah-vor-eh*
waitress	**cameriera**	*kah-mair-ee-air-ah*
waiter	**cameriere**	*kah-mair-ee-aireh*
fixed price menu	**il menù a prezzo fisso**	*eel meh-noo ah pret-soh fee-soh*
dish of the day	**piatto del giorno**	*pee-ah-toh dell jor-no*
starter	**antipasto**	*an-tee-pass-toh*
first course	**il primo**	*eel pree-moh*
main course	**il secondo**	*eel seh-kon-doh*
vegetables	**contorni**	*eel kon-tor-noh*
dessert	**il dolce**	*eel doll-cheh*
cover charge	**il coperto**	*eel koh-pair-toh*
wine list	**la lista dei vini**	*lah lee-stah day vee-nee*
glass	**il bicchiere**	*eel bee-kee-air-eh*
bottle	**la bottiglia**	*lah bot-teel-yah*
knife	**il coltello**	*eel kol-tell-oh*
fork	**la forchetta**	*lah for-ket-tah*
spoon	**il cucchiaio**	*eel koo-kee-eye-oh*

Menu Decoder

l'acqua minerale	*lah-kwah mee-nair-ah-leh*	mineral water
gassata/ naturale	*gah-zah-tah/ nah-too-rah-leh*	fizzy/still
agnello	*ah-niell-oh*	lamb
aglio	*al-ee-oh*	garlic
al forno	*al for-noh*	baked
alla griglia	*ah-lah greel-yah*	grilled
arrosto	*ar-ross-toh*	roast
la birra	*lah beer-rah*	beer
la bistecca	*lah bee-stek-kah*	steak
il burro	*eel boor-oh*	butter
il caffè	*eel kah-feh*	coffee
la carne	*la kar-neh*	meat
carne di maiale	*kar-neh dee mah-yah-leh*	pork
la cipolla	*la chip-oh-lah*	onion
i fagioli	*ee fah-joh-lee*	beans
il formaggio	*eel for-mad-joh*	cheese
le fragole	*leh frah-goh-leh*	strawberries
il fritto misto	*eel free-toh mees-toh*	mixed fried dish
la frutta	*la froot-tah*	fruit
frutta di mare	*froo-tee dee mah-reh*	seafood
i funghi	*ee foon-ghee*	mushrooms
i gamberi	*ee gam-bair-ee*	prawns
il gelato	*eel jel-ah-toh*	ice cream
l'insalata	*leen-sah-lah-tah*	salad
il latte	*eel laht-teh*	milk
lesso	*less-oh*	boiled
il manzo	*eel man-tsoh*	beef
l'olio	*loh-lee-oh*	oil
il pane	*eel pah-neh*	bread
le patate	*leh pah-tah-teh*	potatoes
le patatine fritte	*leh pah-tah-teen-eh free-teh*	chips
il pepe	*eel peh-peh*	pepper
il pesce	*eel pesh-eh*	fish
il pollo	*eel poll-oh*	chicken
il pomodoro	*eel poh-moh-dor-oh*	tomato
il prosciutto cotto/crudo	*eel pro-shoo-toh kot-toh/kroo-doh*	ham cooked/cured
il riso	*eel ree-zoh*	rice
il sale	*eel sah-leh*	salt
la salsiccia	*lah sal-see-chah*	sausage
succo d'arancia/ di limone	*soo-koh dah-ran-chah/ dee lee-moh-neh*	orange/lemon juice
il tè	*eel teh*	tea
la torta	*lah tor-tah*	cake/tart
l'uovo	*loo-oh-voh*	egg
vino bianco	*vee-noh bee-ang-koh*	white wine
vino rosso	*vee-noh ross-oh*	red wine
il vitello	*eel vee-tell-oh*	veal
le vongole	*leh von-goh-leh*	clams
lo zucchero	*loh zoo-kair-oh*	sugar
la zuppa	*lah tsoo-pah*	soup

Numbers

1	**uno**	*oo-noh*
2	**due**	*doo-eh*
3	**tre**	*treh*
4	**quattro**	*kwat-roh*
5	**cinque**	*ching-kweh*
6	**sei**	*say-ee*
7	**sette**	*set-teh*
8	**otto**	*ot-toh*
9	**nove**	*noh-veh*
10	**dieci**	*dee-eh-chee*
11	**undici**	*oon-dee-chee*
12	**dodici**	*doh-dee-chee*
13	**tredici**	*tray-dee-chee*
14	**quattordici**	*kwat-tor-dee-chee*
15	**quindici**	*kwin-dee-chee*
16	**sedici**	*say-dee-chee*
17	**diciassette**	*dee-chah-set-the*
18	**diciotto**	*dee-chot-toh*
19	**diciannove**	*dee-chah-noh-veh*
20	**venti**	*ven-tee*
30	**trenta**	*tren-tah*
40	**quaranta**	*kwah-ran-tah*
50	**cinquanta**	*ching-kwan-tah*
60	**sessanta**	*sess-an-tah*
70	**settanta**	*set-tan-tah*
80	**ottanta**	*ot-tan-tah*
90	**novanta**	*noh-van-tah*
100	**cento**	*chen-toh*
1,000	**mille**	*mee-leh*
2,000	**duemila**	*doo-eh mee-lah*
1,000,000	**un milione**	*oon meel-yoh-neh*

Time

one minute	**un minuto**	*oon mee-noo-toh*
one hour	**un'ora**	*oon or-ah*
a day	**un giorno**	*oon jor-noh*
Monday	**lunedì**	*loo-neh-dee*
Tuesday	**martedì**	*mar-teh-dee*
Wednesday	**mercoledì**	*mair-koh-leh-dee*
Thursday	**giovedì**	*joh-veh-dee*
Friday	**venerdì**	*ven-air-dee*
Saturday	**sabato**	*sah-bah-toh*
Sunday	**domenica**	*doh-meh-nee-kah*

Selected Index